The Inter-American Convention against Corruption

Chapter Two

The Inter-American Convention against Corruption

Annotated with Commentary

by Carlos A. Manfroni

Updated by Richard S. Werksman

Translated by Michael Ford

LEXINGTON BOOKS

Lanham • Boulder • New York • Oxford

LEXINGTON BOOKS

Published in the United States of America
by Lexington Books
A Member of the Rowman & Littlefield Publishing Group
4501 Forbes Boulevard, Suite 200, Lanham, Maryland 20706

PO Box 317
Oxford
OX2 9RU, UK

British Library Cataloguing in Publication Information Available

Library of Congress Cataloging-in-Publication Data

Manfroni, Carlos A.
  [Convenciâon Interamericana Contra la Corrupciâon. English.]
  The Inter-American Convention Against Corruption : annotated with commentary / by Carlos A. Manfroni ; updated by Richard S. Werksman ; translated by Michael Ford.— English language ed.
    p. cm.
  Includes bibliographical references and index.
  ISBN 0-7391-0548-5 (cloth : alk. paper)
  1. Political corruption—America. 2. Bribery—America. 3. Law enforcement—America. I. Inter-American Convention Against Corruption (1996) II. Title.
  KDZ966.M57A3 2003
  341.7'7—dc21   2003000866

Printed in the United States of America

⊗™ The paper used in this publication meets the minimum requirements of American National Standard for Information Sciences—Permanence of Paper for Printed Library Materials, ANSI/NISO Z39.48-1992.

Contents

Foreword to the English Language Edition

"The whole art of government consists in being honest."

—Thomas Jefferson

Democratic leaders in the Americas have begun to fight corruption and impunity as part of a strategy to restore confidence in government and to develop modern economies and fight poverty. The Inter-American Convention against Corruption, one of the most practical and unambiguous anticorruption instruments in the world, is a useful tool to the Western Hemisphere's leaders who want to treat corruption as a crime as well as stop corruption before it occurs.

In twenty-first-century economies based on global trade and competition, the price of corruption or "state-sponsored privilege" is too high for any nation to pay. In modern economies, the "rules of the game" must be applied equally and transparently, without corruption, fear, or favor. When they are, people are more likely to respect the rule of law—"the wise restraints that set men free." Honest courts, equitable regulation, safeguards on property, fair taxation, and reliable public services prime the pump of investment and enterprise and allow persons from all walks of life to claim their fair share of economic opportunity.

In short, anticorruption measures are essential to genuine democracy and development. The Inter-American Convention against Corruption creates legally binding standards that economic partners agree to respect. The Convention's practical value depends on whether it is applied faithfully and systemically, which will generate legal regimes that prosecute abuses, large and small, and cultural norms that stigmatize corruption of any kind.

We can hope that, for the first time, the fight against corruption in the Americas will be comprehensive and sustained. After all, democracy and free enterprise must rest upon the foundation of integrity and honesty. The Convention provides us additional tools to reinforce those values and will be remembered as a seminal document in a stronger and more relevant Inter-American system.

The publication of this book should contribute to the broader understanding and implementation of this important Convention.

Ambassador Roger F. Noriega
United States Permanent Representative
to the Organization of American States
September 2002

Foreword to the First Edition

This work, *The Inter-American Convention against Corruption: Annotated with Commentary*, can be described no more accurately than by the word "pioneering." It is pioneering in being the first publication of its kind to comprehensively discuss the most important legal and institutional aspects of the fight against corruption in the Inter-American environment. And it is also pioneering in having as its central object a convention that is, to date, the only legal instrument applying to this matter: the Inter-American Convention against Corruption, adopted within the framework of the draft for the Specialized Conference on the Inter-American Convention against Corruption held in the city of Caracas on March 29, 1996.

The Inter-American Convention against Corruption, which entered into force on March 6, 1997, almost one year to the day after its conclusion, plays an extremely important role within the Inter-American system, by establishing an indispensable means of cooperation in the international struggle against this scourge, encouraging international activity to prevent, detect, and punish corruption. In fact, corruption is present in our time as a phenomenon of multiple facets, against which measures include actions within both the domestic environment of each country and the external environment in matters of international cooperation; and both spheres are duly covered in this legal instrument.

Within the Organization of American States (OAS), as early as 1992, the Inter-American Juridical Committee was warning of the importance of addressing legal problems originating from the phenomenon of corruption and including the issue on its agenda. At its meeting of April 1994, the same body initially discussed a draft resolution recommending general guidelines for preparing domestic legislation and international agreements, presented by Dr. Luis Herrera Marcano and Dr. Miguel Ángel Espeche Gil.

Meanwhile, on April 21, 1994, the Chilean delegation to the Organization of American States requested that we include on the agenda of the General Assembly the topic "Probity and Civic Ethics." As a consequence of this proposal and of the resulting discussions, the General Assembly adopted resolution 1294 of June 10, 1994, by which it resolved to instruct the Permanent Council to establish a working group that would study the issue. This group, known as the Working Group on Probity and Civic Ethics, was chaired by the Chilean representative to the OAS, Ambassador Edmundo Vargas Carreño, and was responsible for compiling and analyzing current national laws covering public ethics, studying the monitoring and auditing experiences of existing administrative institutions, developing an inventory of offenses relating to public ethics as defined in the national laws, and preparing recommendations on legal mechanisms to monitor the problem of corruption with full respect for the sovereignty of the member states.

Based on the mandate contained in the aforementioned resolution 1294, the Working Group on Probity and Civic Ethics began work by requesting that the organization's member states send it their current national laws relating to public ethics, including criminal laws on offenses against the state.

The Working Group on Probity and Civic Ethics also resolved to hold a seminar, which took place in Montevideo on November 6 and 7, 1995, and which also covered international cooperation against corruption, existing national experiences in this matter, and contributions the private sector might make in this regard.

On December 16, 1994, the Venezuelan government presented a draft convention, which was sent by the Permanent Council to the Working Group, which was in full operation, which in turn sent copies to the member states with a view to collecting comments. In turn, the General Assembly charged Working Group on Probity and Civic Ethics chairman Ambassador Edmundo Vargas Carreño with preparing a draft Inter-American Convention against Corruption based on the Venezuelan proposal, as well as comments made by the governments. It also charged the Inter-American Juridical Committee with providing comments on the draft convention prepared by the Working Group. Finally, the Assembly decided to call for the participation of experts to discuss the draft and comments originating from the various sources mentioned above.

Subsequent meetings of experts, held in Washington, D.C., culminated in the Specialized Conference of Caracas, which adopted the final text of the Inter-American Convention against Corruption.

One of the most important milestones illustrating the OAS's concern in this area was the Summit of the Americas, held in December 1994, at which the hemisphere's presidents and heads of state discussed the fight against corruption as a priority of the Inter-American agenda and as contributing to strengthening representative democracy in our countries, an indispensable condition for regional stability, peace, and development. The OAS therefore came to be an important action center for adopting the measures needed to perfect the mechanisms of international cooperation against this complex problem.

The Summit's final document stated that effective democracy requires that corruption be combated holistically, since it is a factor of social disintegration and distortion of the economic system, which undermines the legitimacy of political institutions. This notion was developed over the years in the works of the OAS.

From the Summit of the Americas to the present day, and in response to that call, the OAS not only has adopted the Inter-American Convention against Corruption but also has approved the Inter-American Program for Cooperation in the Fight against Corruption. And it has undertaken work with a view to preparing model legislation, for purposes of classifying certain acts of corruption and specific activities for cooperation in this field.

The pattern followed by both the Convention and the Inter-American Program was to recognize that the actions states need to take must be approached both from a legal standpoint and from an institutional standpoint, without ignoring the participative mechanisms of civil society and nongovernmental organizations, as well as close collaboration with international agencies that perform important tasks in combating corruption, such as the United Nations, the Council of Europe, the Organization for Economic Cooperation and Development, the World Bank, the International Monetary Fund, and the Inter-American Development Bank.

To this end, the convention dedicates several of its provisions to implementing preventive measures with multiple effects on the administrative law of the separate states, to standards for notification, to measures for the gradual development and harmonization of domestic legal systems, to mechanisms for extradition, forfeiture, and distribution of forfeited property, to the functioning of central authorities, etc. In addition, as demonstrated during the course of this work, the Inter-American Convention against Corruption has the virtue of establishing the notion of mandatory assistance and cooperation between the states that is not contingent upon petitions from judges or the filing of a legal proceeding, as well as requiring the lifting of bank secrecy.

The Inter-American Program for Cooperation in the Fight against Corruption, which appears in the appendix of this work, also touches upon the four aforementioned areas, emphasizing the participation of civil society and nongovernmental organizations. It is here that we see the most interesting and — why not say it? — innovative aspect of the Inter-American Program. In effect, information campaigns on the Inter-American Convention against Corruption are anticipated in the communications media, consideration is being given to participation by the press, bar associations, auditors, and accountants, and efforts are being made to promote disclosure of the ethical values on which the fight against corruption is based.

This book globally and completely touches upon each and every one of these points, and offers a wider perspective on the implementation of these legal instruments in the future.

I do not wish to close without expressing my pleasure at having had the opportunity to make these comments on the purpose of the work by Dr. Carlos Manfroni and Dr. Richard Werksman. As Assistant Secretary for Legal Affairs of the Organization of American States, I believe that the dissemination of continentwide legal thinking, in this case on the fight against corruption, is one of the activities that must be addressed with the greatest determination and perseverance, not only by those of us who work in the General Secretariat of that organization, but by all admirers of international law. This task cannot be in better hands at this time than in those of Carlos Manfroni and Richard Werksman, for whom I feel tremendous professional respect, and who, with their knowledge of the topic in question, will most certainly provide an invaluable study and work tool for everyone who has the opportunity to read this publication.

Enrique Lagos
Assistant Secretary for Legal Affairs
Organization of American States

Preface to the English Language Edition

This volume is an updated, English language translation of "La Convencion Interamericana Contra la Corrupcion, Anotada y Comentada," published by Abeledo-Perrot in Buenos Aires, Argentina. The updates concern principally the creation of the Committee of Experts and its activities to assess progress of the states parties to the Convention in meeting their obligations to fight corruption under the Inter-American Convention against Corruption. The Committee was created in 2001 under the Document of Buenos Aires, an agreement the twenty-seven states ratifying parties to the Convention have adopted as a mutual review mechanism. It met twice in 2002 to begin the first round of the assessment process, which is described in detail in chapter 4.

While the Convention itself has not been amended or modified since its adoption in 1966, the Document of Buenos Aires and the Committee of Experts represent an important enhancement of the Convention and the commitment of its ratifiers to fulfill their obligations under it.

Other updates include additional appendixes pertinent to the Convention and recent changes to several of the appendixes to the original publication, including the list of states parties that have ratified the Convention. The most recent ratifiers are Brazil and Suriname.

New appendixes include the Rules of the Committee of Experts and a list of Websites for the most current information about the Convention in particular and the struggle against corruption in Latin America.

Preface to the First Edition

The Inter-American Convention against Corruption is an international legal instrument that is new both because of its specific content and because of its very nature, since this is the first time that a hemispherewide standard has been created to regulate a matter that, until now, had been strictly the preserve of domestic law.

The unusually high number of countries that signed the document in Caracas is evidence that the Convention is something more than a paper written with good intentions. It addresses a firm and current complaint of the peoples of the Americas, who are no longer content merely to hear fine words from their governing authorities.

In this book, we attempt to offer an explanation of the agreement, which focuses also on the historical perspective of the discussions of the working group in which we were honored to participate. We therefore hope to provide a useful instrument for interpreting a supranational standard that is intended, as such, to form part of the positive law of all the states parties.

It would be very difficult to thank every one of the members of the OAS, the governments of the hemisphere, and the Inter-American Juridical Committee, with whom we have shared so many pleasant hours of discussion and analysis in Washington, D.C., and Caracas. We will therefore limit our expressions of thanks—though without limiting our gratitude—to Dr. César Gaviria Trujillo, Ambassador Edmundo Vargas Carreño, Dr. Enrique Lagos, Ambassador Alicia Martínez Ríos, Ambassador Harriet C. Babbitt, Minister José Ureta, and Dr. Peter Quilter, among the authorities of the Organization of American States and the members of the delegations of our countries of origin, as well as Fundación BankBoston of Argentina, its president, Manuel Sacerdote, and its executive director, Dr. Enrique

Morad, for the support they consistently provided in disseminating these materials. This acknowledgement contains our friendly greetings to the men and women from every government of the Americas, and from civil society organizations, who made possible the Inter-American Convention against Corruption.

Chapter One

Why Combat Corruption Internationally?

If, a few years before the signing of the Inter-American Convention against Corruption, someone had suggested that corruption is an evil that should be fought using international tools, not only governments but also, perhaps, most people would have reacted negatively.

The popular expression "dirty laundry should be washed at home" is not unrelated to politics. National pride, worthy of better causes, has on numerous occasions served corrupt governments and demagogues, allowing them to gain undeserved support from the people whom they themselves were swindling.

Not a few domestic companies wrap themselves in their national colors to evade the commercial competition that would require them to reduce the excess costs they charge states, which thus constitute a burden for their citizens.

Lack of communications, inflation, economic confusion, and the need to fight terrorism have obscured the problem of corruption. But the problem was always there; at times, as the source of some of those evils, at other times, as an unprovable but unfortunately effective excuse in favor of those causing them.

The people's openness toward greater knowledge of the planet, the disappearance of the Cold War, and the decline in terrorism, as well as the adjustments that many countries in Latin America were required to make to halt inflation and bankruptcy, resulted in increased awareness among the people of the seriousness of the problem and its impact on the way of life of each and every one of those who suffer from poverty or limitations.

Fiscal discipline allows us to calculate numbers and verify how much money is not getting through to health, education, justice, and defense, as a result of corruption.

Communications satellites have carried to every corner of the world images of the standards of living of developed countries.

Domestic and external peace have allowed the dosage of combativeness that every person carries within himself to be channeled toward greater demands on governments.

Within this context, the annual meeting of the countries comprising the Rio Group, in the city of Quito, in October 1994, was dedicated to the issue of "Modernization of the State and Administrative Probity." At this congress, the representatives of various states combined their experience on ways to combat corruption. One month later, the United States Information Agency and the United States Office of Government Ethics organized the First International Conference on Ethics in Government, in the city of Washington, D.C., with representatives of more than fifty countries. But it was in December of that same year, in Miami, that the Summit of the Americas for the first time publicly launched the idea of combating corruption internationally.

However, that idea had been included on the agenda of the Inter-American Juridical Committee two years earlier at the initiative of one of its members, Argentine legal expert Jorge Reinaldo Vanossi. In a study published in his country in 1992, he had proposed treating corruption as an international problem and anticipated the needs of some of the institutions that later adopted the convention, such as penalizing transnational bribery, lifting bank secrecy, and preventing political asylum from being used by corrupt politicians to avoid accountability.

In 1995, Venezuela put forth a proposal that, among other new measures, contained a commitment to grant extradition of corrupt officials. This plan by President Caldera was taken up by the Organization of American States, which formed the Working Group on Probity and Civic Ethics, headed by Chilean ambassador to the OAS Edmundo Vargas Carreño, which together with the Secretariat dedicated itself to preparing a document that would give rise to a convention. In this task it had the assistance of the Inter-American Juridical Committee, which offered its opinion, support, and constructive criticism through a working group comprising Drs. Luis Herrera Marcano, Eduardo Vío Grossi, and Rapporteur-Chairman Miguel A. Espeche Gil.

After collecting the basic materials, the Organization of American States convoked a meeting of experts from all countries of the Americas, who were responsible for preparing the draft that was to become the Inter-American Convention against Corruption (ICAC), over the course of several months of subsequent meetings in Washington, D.C.

The work came to an end on March 29, 1996, when twenty-one countries signed the document in Caracas.

However, having noted these causes and this summary sequence, the first questions come to mind: Why must corruption be combated internationally? Why have the commitments been condensed into an international instrument when, until a few years ago, the government authorities claimed they maintained such a contract only with their own people?

We have identified seven reasons why corruption must be combated internationally. There will most certainly be several more. All of them are reflected in the preamble to the ICAC, which we discuss further in chapter 2. We believe that these reasons are sufficient to justify the activity and interest of the international community.

1. Corruption is too sensitive an issue for the government authorities to leave those who are governed unprotected in the face of a complete lack of interest on the part of the international community.
2. Liberalization requires transparency, as a safeguard of justice and fairness in economic exchanges between nations.
3. Encouragement must be given to peace and the development of people, who are being harassed by the unfair burdens of corruption, which in turn provides the excuse for the most violent and seditious groups to attack institutions.
4. The fight against corruption is a means of preserving the legitimacy of institutions and systems, which are undermined by illegitimate practices when not governed for the common good.
5. It is necessary to fight organized crime and drug trafficking, for which international cooperation is necessary.
6. Broader international cooperation is needed to obtain information, evidence, and extradition.
7. Greater ethical awareness and a higher degree of protection for individuals with the vocation and determination to combat corruption must be generated among civil society.

These arguments will be developed in the comments to the preamble of the Inter-American Convention against Corruption.

The Inter-American Convention against Corruption

Section-by-Section Text, Analysis, and Commentary

PREAMBLE

THE MEMBER STATES OF THE ORGANIZATION OF AMERICAN STATES, CONVINCED *that corruption undermines the legitimacy of public institutions and strikes at society, moral order and justice, as well as at the comprehensive development of peoples;*

CONSIDERING *that representative democracy, an essential condition for stability, peace and development of the region, requires, by its nature, the combating of every form of corruption in the performance of public functions, as well as acts of corruption specifically related to such performance;*

PERSUADED *that fighting corruption strengthens democratic institutions and prevents distortions in the economy, improprieties in government and damage to a society's moral fiber;*

RECOGNIZING *that corruption is often a tool used by organized crime for the accomplishment of its purposes;*

CONVINCED *of the importance of making people in the countries of the region aware of this problem and its gravity, and of the need to strengthen participation by civil society in preventing and fighting corruption;*

RECOGNIZING *that, in some cases, corruption has international dimensions, which requires coordinated action by States to fight it effectively;*

CONVINCED *of the need for prompt adoption of an international instrument to promote and facilitate international cooperation in fighting corruption and, especially, in taking appropriate action against persons who undertake acts of corruption in the performance of public functions, or acts specifically related to such performance, as well as appropriate measures with respect to the proceeds of such acts;*

DEEPLY CONCERNED by the steadily increasing links between corruption and the proceeds generated by illicit narcotics trafficking which undermine and threaten lawful commercial and financial activities, and society, at all levels;

BEARING IN MIND the responsibility of States to hold corrupt persons accountable in order to combat corruption and to cooperate with one another for their efforts in this area to be effective; and

DETERMINED to make every effort to prevent, detect, punish and eradicate corruption in the performance of public functions and acts of corruption specifically related to such performance,

HAVE AGREED to adopt the following
Inter-American Convention against Corruption

As may be seen, the reasons that make international cooperation necessary to fight corruption are clearly expressed in the preamble, the drafting of which was left until the end of the Washington meeting. For methodological reasons, we will not comment on the preamble in the order of its paragraphs, but rather in accordance with the connection of its statements to the causes of the need for international efforts in the fight against corruption.

An Issue Too Sensitive for Governments

There are certain issues that are so sensitive for governments that the international community cannot fail to notice them. Corruption is one of these evils that claims a certain level of international notice, because corrupt officials weaken the structures of their own states and it is therefore necessary to gain a multilateral commitment by which the governing authorities consent to a certain degree of interaction with their peers from other nations.

Reality is not always so simple that it may be summarized as a lack of absolute will to control corruption on the part of the authorities. In certain cases, governments see themselves as hemmed in by the nets that corruption has woven around them, and only an international commitment can offer their officials the support and motives to free themselves from the ties that many of their structures maintain with the worst interests.

This is what is meant, among other things, by the ICAC preamble when it refers to "the need for prompt adoption of an international instrument to promote and facilitate international cooperation in fighting corruption and, especially, in taking appropriate action against persons who undertake acts of corruption in the performance of public functions, or acts specifically related to such performance," as well as when it notes "the responsibility of States to hold corrupt persons accountable in order to combat corruption and to cooperate with one another for their efforts in this area to be effective."

Liberalization Requires Transparency

Relations between nations are increasingly close and, at the same time, open. One of the primary engines of trade today is the communications to which we previously referred, as well as economics. Comparisons made through such trade promote cost reductions even though, at times, there is also a need for undesired adjustments.

Nevertheless, certain evils attributed to excess liberalization originate rather from distortions in the system, because of competition that, rather than being open and transparent, is unfair. And one of the forms of this unfairness is corruption.

Corruption holds the market hostage within a country and penetrates that market from other countries using weapons that have nothing to do with the price and quality of the products sold. At the same time, legal security disappears because the lawmakers and courts do not exercise their power for the common good but rather to the benefit of those who paid them bribes. This, then, generates deep mistrust in trade and an absence of fairness that harms those who fairly compete in the market.

The preamble refers to this and to other realities when it states, "in some cases, corruption has international dimensions, which requires coordinated action by States to fight it effectively."

The parties most harmed by this situation are the people, who are thereby deterred in their opportunities for development.

Promotion of Peace and Development of the People

When a state fails to offer legal security, not only do investors not go to its territory, but in addition, the country's own sound domestic capital emigrates to other countries, in search of better conditions for promoting worthy companies, or simply to be safeguarded in bank accounts. In social terms, this means fewer sources of employment.

Added to the unemployment that sometimes occurs to a certain degree because of the scarcity of resources or the substitution of labor, there is the poverty that results when these circumstances are combined with government corruption, which drives out investment and misallocates funds intended to alleviate the effects of unemployment and poverty.

Such situations have often resulted in mass unrest or have served as an excuse for subversive groups to promote chaos and anarchy. For this reason, the preamble of the ICAC states, "representative democracy, an essential condition for stability, peace and development of the region, requires, by its nature, the combating of every form of corruption in the performance of public functions, as well as acts of corruption specifically related to such performance."

Preserving the Legitimacy of Institutions and Systems

Corruption not only harms the economy, impedes development, and generates unrest and poverty, which is already enough. It also discredits the country's institutions and freedom itself as a system of international coexistence. Not a few people, in various communities around the world, claim that they lived better when they were slaves to a totalitarian regime than when they were freed from that type of oppression. It is for this reason that people's morale declines, that because of permanent mistrust in politics they abandon all forms of control, allowing themselves to be dragged down by indifference and even to pervert their own personal customs, given the absence of a temporal system of rewards and punishments.

The preamble recognizes these circumstances when it notes that "fighting corruption strengthens democratic institutions and prevents distortions in the economy, improprieties in government and damage to a society's moral fiber." But at the same time, that introduction recognizes a principle of natural law, that authorities require legitimacy regarding their origin as well as their actions. Corruption undermines authority in its exercise, because "corruption undermines the legitimacy of public institutions and strikes at society, moral order and justice, as well as at the comprehensive development of peoples."

Combating Organized Crime

There is a great deal of concern for the links between corruption and organized crime, mafias within and outside the governments, and the profusion of drug trafficking, one of the greatest evils of our time.

On some occasions, corruption is caused by these true factors of illegitimate power; on others, it is precisely these powers that best take advantage of corruption already existing in the governments to expand their businesses and take over institutions.

Organized crime is not an evil that can be fought by one country alone. It involves forces too powerful and too contaminating for their confrontation not to be the responsibility of the entire international community. In this regard, it is somewhat similar to the case of the environment: if one party cleans and cares for it but his neighbor does not, the cleaning and care that the first party performed does little good. Within a short period of time, everything becomes dirty again. The preamble acknowledges this reality when it states, "corruption is often a tool used by organized crime for the accomplishment of its purposes." And it also notes the profound concern of the states at "the steadily increasing links between corruption and the proceeds generated by illicit narcotics trafficking which undermine and threaten lawful commercial and financial activities, and society, at all levels."

International Cooperation

It is not only organized crime, but also common offenses of corruption against the government that require international cooperation. All too frequently, corrupt officials take such measures as hiding their property in other countries or fleeing abroad to avoid legal proceedings. International assistance and cooperation are basic requirements for obtaining information, collecting evidence, seeking property, detecting "laundering," and processing extraditions.

The ICAC has contributed innovative solutions in all these areas as well as many others related to international cooperation. In providing these solutions, the preamble notes "the responsibility of States to hold corrupt persons accountable in order to combat corruption and to cooperate with one another for their efforts in this area to be effective."

To this end, the states undertake "to make every effort to prevent, detect, punish and eradicate corruption in the performance of public functions and acts of corruption specifically related to such performance."

Preventing corruption is the most important of these activities, because it seeks to prevent illegal acts from occurring.

Such prevention is more closely linked to systems than to people, more to causes than to effects. In general, it is also more closely linked to administrative law than to criminal law. For this reason, the benefits of any preventive mechanisms that are established, if they are appropriate, will always be greater than the benefits of applying penalties.

The above statements must not be taken to mean a conflict between preventive and punitive measures, because punitive systems also serve for preventive purposes, and without them, the best preventive systems run the risk of becoming loose. It is simply necessary to take into consideration the fact that, if one looks only at quantity, one may see that there are more cases of corruption prevented through a system that offers fewer opportunities for crime than there are cases avoided through the example—of all types, always positive—of a well-applied penalty.

The importance given to prevention by the convention was reflected in the position assigned to the long article on "preventive measures," number III, immediately after the statements we have been discussing here. Detecting corruption is a matter in which international responsibility plays a basic role.

As an anecdotal issue, one might note the case of the word "eradication," which many members of the group of experts challenged because they believed the idea of eradicating corruption to be too presumptuous. Nevertheless, it was decided to keep it, since it refers to an ultimate goal, a guideline for all intermediate steps that might be taken toward achieving perfection, even given the limitations of real life.

The inclusion of the phrase "specifically related to such performance" referred to a very prudent proposal by Peru, that beginning with the preamble itself, the scope of the convention should cover not only acts by public officials, but also those by private individuals who encourage or participate in corruption.

Increasing Awareness and Protecting Individuals

Civil society's participation in monitoring governments is a development of the most modern form of administration. Citizens play a fundamental role in both preventing corruption and detecting its effects. But for this participation to be possible to a significant degree, two requirements are necessary:

1. Transparency laws must be promoted to allow citizens to be knowledgeable of government acts.
2. Citizens determined to fight corruption must receive protection for their lives, their physical, moral, and economic well-being, and their right to engage in their respective activities. For this reason, the ICAC operates as a safeguard, as a "human rights" agreement that warns governments that citizens who challenge corruption are not alone, but rather that their voices may be heard throughout the entire international community. To this end, the preamble maintains "the need for prompt adoption of an international instrument to promote and facilitate international cooperation in fighting corruption and, especially, in taking appropriate action against persons who undertake acts of corruption in the performance of public functions, or acts specifically related to such performance, as well as appropriate measures with respect to the proceeds of such acts."

ARTICLE I

DEFINITIONS

For the purposes of this Convention:

"Public function" means any temporary or permanent, paid or honorary activity, performed by a natural person in the name of the State or in the service of the State or its institutions, at any level of its hierarchy.

"Public official", "government official", or "public servant" means any official or employee of the State or its agencies, including those who have been selected, appointed, or elected to perform activities or functions in the name of the State or in the service of the State, at any level of its hierarchy.

"Property" means assets of any kind, whether movable or immovable, tangible or intangible, and any document or legal instrument demonstrating, purporting to demonstrate, or relating to ownership or other rights pertaining to such assets.

Some Difficulties in the Convention's Definitions

The text of the convention begins by defining certain terms used in the document. This issue, which is at first glance simple, generated some difficulties during the ICAC negotiations, particularly because of the diversity of cultures of the member countries and the consequent difference of meaning or scope between certain legal concepts. This fact, combined with the need to precisely understand the words that needed to be defined, was the basis for the discussion of article I toward the end of the negotiations, to such an extent that it was not discussed in Caracas until the day prior to the instrument's signing, and was not drafted in any of the three rounds held in Washington, D.C.

Nevertheless, only a few terms are covered by the definitions. These are expressions whose interpretation might generate some problem in applying the commitment. In fact, these concepts are limited to three: "public function," "public official" (and its synonyms), and "property."

The first difference of opinion among the drafters focused on the alternative of focusing priority on "public function" or "public official," in such a way that the definition of one of these concepts would make it unnecessary to define the other. Certain countries, however, because of their systems for approving international documents, which are examined by a large number of government agencies before signing, insisted on the need to make explicit reference both to "public function" and to "public official," even at the risk of a tautology.

Semantic differences, not only between nations of different language but also between countries of the same language, and the diversity of legal cultures prevented—unfortunately—the drafting of definitions that would have resulted in models of precision, as would have been desirable, given the document's importance. In any case, the definitions appear to be acceptable and the general nature of their text will prevent an excessively restrictive interpretation.

Public Function

The most serious problem in the description of "public function" arose from the need to find a basic common denominator that did not exclude any type of activity that was to be covered by the convention. It was necessary that both elective positions and political appointments be covered by the article's stipulations. The same applied to paid and honorary activities, temporary or permanent. These definitions were explicitly set forth in the portion of the article that reads: "any temporary or permanent, paid or honorary activity, performed by a natural person in the name of the State or in the service of the State or its institutions, at any level of its hierarchy."

As may be seen, however, the inclusion of the qualities temporary, permanent, paid, or honorary is descriptive. The core of the definition consists of three concepts: (1) activity; (2) natural person; and (3) in the name of the state or in the service of the state.

The word "activity" refers to the provision of a service, even if temporary. It is important to distinguish this situation from outsourcing a job, even when the work is assigned to a natural person.

We therefore believe that if a government contracts to a consultant to issue reports during the year, about various situations affecting a certain area, that consultant is a public official.

By contrast, if a government were to assign a project or a report on a specific issue, the author does not become a public official, but rather is a supplier to the state.

This is logical, because in outsourcing a job, the provider has only an obligation of result. By contrast, when leasing out services, the principal obligation is the activity itself, as requested by the ICAC. We cannot imagine that an architect who delivers to the state a plan for an airport becomes a public official for that reason. But we can indeed imagine that this would apply to an architect engaged to evaluate an indeterminate number of projects, over a certain period of time.

The reference to natural person contributes to excluding the remote, although not unlikely, extension of the notion of public function to the activity of a licensee (a related proposal came up during the discussions).

The phrase "in the name of the State or in the service of the State" allows coverage both of activities by the highest authorities of the three branches of the republic—or others carried out on the state's behalf by delegation—as well as of activities of subordinates, carried out in service to the state.

A president, a legislator, and a judge are acting in the name of the state. The same cannot be said for any employee of a state agency who does not directly claim state power.

It would have been preferable, and this is what we proposed during the discussions, for the definition to read, for all cases, simply: "all activities carried out by a natural person, in the service of the interests of the State." This would have afforded greater precision to the definition of "service," since this term, without the word "interests," may cover, for example, activities by a licensee that does not perform a public function.

The word "interests" further limits the category, since in a democratic and capitalist system only those who perform a public function may act in the service of the interests of the state. All other participants, such as licensees, as the case may be, are working in their own interests. By contrast, members of certain professional corporations who in some countries perform functions corresponding to the state, such as record keeping, legal experts, and other private parties, depending upon the law in each of the states parties, work in the interests of the state, even if they are not public officials. These persons should therefore be covered by the convention's commitments.

In any case, the noun "natural person" prevents an excessive extension of the phrase "in the service of the State," as we previously noted. Also the expression: "at any level of its hierarchy" supports the accuracy of the definition, since only a person who performs a public function can have a hierarchical level.

Finally, when we speak of the state or of its other entities, it is an attempt to include companies that remain within the state orbit or autarchic or decentralized agencies, as may be seen.

Public Official, Government Official, Public Servant

The differences in some countries as to the scope of the definition of public official made it necessary to compare that term with government official and public servant, for purposes of the convention.

The paragraph appears to be a mere repeat of notions contained in the definition of public function. And this is partially the case. But the definition of public official, despite the aforementioned methodological difficulties, contributes essential information to understanding the convention.

The first new items consists, as noted, in the comparison of certain terms that do not have the same meaning in all countries. The expression "public official," for example, is reserved by a certain administrative terminology to employees with decision-making power over state matters. It does not therefore include employees whose tasks involve advising or assistance, or whose duties are simply not decisive for the establishment of an administrative, legislative, or legal act, subject, of course, to trends of opinion.

The will of the convention's authors was not aimed at limiting the scope of the document in that way, such that, to eliminate all doubt, the definition might make the terms "public official," "government official," and "public servant" comparable

The criteria that was followed is undoubtedly the best. It would not have been fair or prudent to apply the convention solely to the highest level officials or those with decision-making power for issuing administrative, legislative, or legal acts. Acts of corruption are often carried out by lower hierarchy employees who handle files or serve the public, and who may therefore, for example, request a bribe to accelerate a proceeding, or to divert a document to benefit or harm an individual.

The following words contained a tautology, in that a public official is defined as "any official or employee of the State or its agencies."

The extent of the discussions on this article, which lacked a solution satisfactory to all member countries, because of differences in languages and legal cultures, led to this formula, which was considered as being the best one possible under the circumstances. In any event, the tautology is not relevant in this case, for two reasons:

1. In the preceding paragraph of the same article "public function" was already defined in a way that clearly established the notion of public official, by deduction.
2. The principal object of the paragraph on public officials was not to define the nearest category and the specific difference, but rather the need to extend the concept of public official, for purposes of the convention, to those who have been elected or appointed to a position, when they have not yet taken office.

For this reason, the most innovative element of the definition is precisely the phrase that reads "including those who have been selected, appointed, or elected to perform activities or functions in the name of the State or in the service of the State, at any level of its hierarchy."

The novelty, however, does not imply the convention's intent to define public official in heterodox fashion and thereby create a new legal dogma. It is simply an agreement with respect to the extension of the effects of the convention. For this reason, before the definitions the article reads: "For the purposes of this Convention, [term] means. . . ."

Once the aforementioned definition is taken into consideration, it may be noted that the clause, whose final effects very probably might pass unnoticed in a swift reading of the convention, has truly "revolutionary" consequences for criminal law in the signatory countries. This is the case because article VII of the convention requires that states parties adopt "the necessary legislative or other measures to establish as criminal offenses under their domestic law the acts of corruption described in Article VI(1) and to facilitate cooperation among themselves pursuant to this Convention."

Among the acts of corruption described in article VI(1) are bribery, both active and passive, and fraudulent administration. Both must be committed by a public official or with respect to a public official (in the case of a private individual attempting to bribe a public official).

Since the convention includes in the definition of "public official" those who have been selected, appointed, or elected to occupy a position, even before they take office, the combination of articles I, VI, and VII results in the obligation of the states to extend their classification of crimes of bribery (or equivalent categories) to acts committed by persons covered by the afore-mentioned situation. That is, not only must a bribe offered or granted to some-one performing a public position be punished, but so also must be one offered or granted to a person appointed, selected, or elected to hold that position, even if he has not yet assumed office.

Certainly, the classification of crimes must include both the official and the private party who bribed him or attempted to bribe him.

This provision seeks to cover the frequent case of bribes offered or granted to persons who have not yet assumed office, with a view to performing or omit-ting acts after they assume the office to which they were appointed, selected, or elected. Let us assume, in this case, a judge who has been appointed to that po-sition, and during the period between the appointment and his taking of the oath as a magistrate or at the time he effectively takes charge of his court, he receives a bribe to issue a ruling in favor of the individual who offered the bribe.

There are, unfortunately, numerous private interests seeking to influence the state authorities through acts of corruption aimed at the will of those as-signed to perform duties in the near future.

For this reason, it would be desirable for the obligation to punish bribery aimed at future acts to be covered more explicitly in future expansions of the convention. A more committed strategy would even provide for those stipu-lations to be extended to bribes received by political candidates, when they have not yet even been elected to the public office to which they have been nominated by their parties, since compromising the will of future officials is quite frequent during the course of electoral campaigns.

By contrast, the commitment to establish classifications of crimes for offi-cials who have not yet assumed office, by its very nature, cannot be extended to the offense of state fraud, because this offense would never be able to be committed by someone not performing his functions, unless it involved par-ticipation (complicity); but in this case it would not be necessary to make a change to the positive legal structures of the signatory countries, all of which include mechanisms for establishing and applying penalties to participants.

Property

During meetings to prepare the text of the convention, there were discussions regarding the usefulness of the definition of "property," for purposes of the document, since all countries have uniform definitions of this term, through definitions in their laws or their legal traditions.

The position of those who claimed that such a definition was useless ap-pears to be strengthened by the first words of the text that was approved in the end: "assets of any kind, whether movable or immovable, tangible or in-tangible."

However, the argument that finalized the inclusion of a definition in the document was one that supported the need to eliminate any doubts as to the extent of the convention's applicability to certain items important for an investigation. Such items, as noted in the last part of the article, are "any document or legal instrument demonstrating, purporting to demonstrate, or relating to ownership or other rights pertaining to such assets."

This definition is particularly relevant to article XV of the convention, which requires that states parties provide "the widest possible measure of assistance in the identification, tracing, freezing, seizure and forfeiture of property or proceeds obtained, derived from or used in the commission of offenses established in accordance with this Convention."

The definition is also useful for supplementing shortfalls in some articles that do not expressly refer to money but rather to objects of monetary value. The definition of property, in referring to property of any kind, whether movable or immovable, tangible or intangible, makes the convention more precise.

ARTICLE II

PURPOSES

The purposes of this Convention are:

1. *To promote and strengthen the development by each of the States Parties of the mechanisms needed to prevent, detect, punish and eradicate corruption; and*
2. *To promote, facilitate and regulate cooperation among the States Parties to ensure the effectiveness of measures and actions to prevent, detect, punish and eradicate corruption in the performance of public functions and acts of corruption specifically related to such performance.*

General Information

In any legal instrument, a definition of purpose is crucial for interpreting the standards contained in the document. In the case of the convention, the purposes were so important that, despite their position in article II, their drafting was put off until the end of the Washington discussions.

When considering the goals of a document of this type, one must take into account the fact that a convention does not necessarily need to be innovative with respect to the positive law of each of the signatory countries. Conventions are drafted primarily to strengthen the current provisions in the signing states, to create an international network that increases the possibility of real application of those standards, and to establish a system of cooperation that deters or discourages impunity.

However, the Inter-American Convention against Corruption is innovative in many aspects that are not taken into consideration in the positive law of the member states, as we see throughout this book.

The essence of the convention is summarized in sections 1 and 2, article II.

Prevent, Detect, Punish, and Eradicate

As may be clearly seen, the purpose of the article's two sections is to prevent, detect, punish, and eradicate corruption; in the first, by promoting and strengthening mechanisms in each of the states parties; in the second, through cooperation between the states parties.

Regarding the scope of the terms "prevent," "detect," "punish," and "eradicate," we will refer to our statements in the comments to the preamble.

Mechanisms of the States Parties

The words "promote" and "strengthen" at the beginning of section 1 of the article in question relate to our observations in the general information section of this chapter.

As may be seen, they refer to promoting and strengthening mechanisms, i.e., systems and legal and regulatory procedures in each of the states parties.

The promotion of mechanisms relates to the convention's innovative purposes with respect to the positive law applying in each of the signatory countries. Strengthening, by contrast, refers to international solidarity aimed at increasing the effectiveness of those mechanisms. Such strengthening is particularly necessary in the case of standards that may, in theory, affect precisely those responsible for ensuring their enforcement, which are governments. This may occur, for example, in matters of human rights as well as corruption.

Indeed, it is precisely government officials who are capable of committing human rights violations, in the international legal sense of the term. Corruption, by its very nature, also requires activity by a state agent. This special circumstance is what has led the international community to turn its attention toward activities by states, to seek a strengthening of the basic human rights of individuals and communities.

Inter-American Cooperation

Section 2 of article II states the purpose as being to promote, facilitate, and regulate cooperation among the states parties.

In this context, the word "promote" has the sense of encouraging cooperation through a commitment entered into by the states in the convention. Such
cooperation is also facilitated by that very commitment and by the regulation
of such obligation as stipulated in the text. The term "regulate" in this section
refers to the setting of specific rules to which the states parties must be subject in their duty to cooperate, e.g., information on evidence, information on
property acquired as a consequence of a corrupt act, the seizing of such property, extradition, the impossibility of claiming bank secrecy, etc.

ARTICLE III

PREVENTIVE MEASURES[1]

*For the purposes set forth in Article II of this Convention, the States Parties
agree to consider the applicability of measures within their own institutional
systems to create, maintain and strengthen:*

1. *Standards of conduct for the correct, honorable, and proper fulfillment of
   public functions. These standards shall be intended to prevent conflicts of interest and mandate the proper conservation and use of resources entrusted
   to government officials in the performance of their functions.*

   *These standards shall also establish measures and systems requiring
   government officials to report to appropriate authorities acts of corruption
   in the performance of public functions.*

   *Such measures should help preserve the public's confidence in the integrity
   of public servants and government processes.*
2. *Mechanisms to enforce these standards of conduct.*
3. *Instruction to government personnel to ensure proper understanding of
   their responsibilities and the ethical standards governing their activities.*
4. *Systems for registering the earnings, property and liabilities of persons
   who perform public functions in certain posts as specified by law and,
   where appropriate, for making such registrations public.*
5. *Systems of government hiring and procurement of goods and services that
   assure the openness, equity and efficiency of such systems.*
6. *Government revenue collection and control systems that deter corruption.*
7. *Laws that refuse favorable tax treatment for any individual or corporation
   for expenditures made in violation of the anticorruption laws of the States
   Parties.*

---

[1] This comment is not copyrighted because its author is a U.S. government official, and because of
that country's laws applying to government agents. Nevertheless, the content represents the author's
opinion and not necessarily the official position of the government of the United States.

8. *Systems for protecting public servants and private citizens who, in good faith, report acts of corruption, including protection of their identities, in accordance with their Constitutions and the basic principles of their domestic legal systems*

9. *Oversight bodies with a view to implementing modern mechanisms for preventing, detecting, punishing and eradicating corrupt acts.*

10. *Deterrents to the bribery of domestic and foreign government officials, such as mechanisms to ensure that publicly held companies and other types of associations maintain books and records which, in reasonable detail, accurately reflect the acquisition and disposition of property, and have sufficient domestic accounting controls to enable their officers to detect corrupt acts.*

11. *Mechanisms to encourage participation by civil society and nongovernmental organizations in efforts to prevent corruption.*

12. *The study of further preventive measures that take into account the relationship between equitable compensation and probity in public service.*

Article III of the convention is different from the other sections of the document in several ways. First, as the title notes, the goal of its various sections is to prevent, rather than punish, corruption. Second, despite the article's indisputable importance, this clause places fewer mandatory obligations on the parties. Third, it places the focus on the administrative, rather than on the criminal area. And fourth, it is more closely related to civil society and the entire population of each state party than other sections of the convention, although like those other sections, it also addresses the conduct and responsibilities of public officials. Finally, the standard centers on two key elements in the fight against corruption: the elimination of impunity by public officials at all levels, and increased transparency in the public sector.

We examine each of these features of article III in more detail, the successful implementation of which, unlike the issues relevant to other sections of the convention, such as extradition, the courts, and criminal proceedings, may contribute a great deal toward the fight against corruption. Because this article has so much to do with honest conduct and the probity of all public officials, and because success in the fight against corruption is linked to increased trust by citizens in the probity of the public sector, implementing this chapter may achieve more results by preventing corruption than by punishing it.

Before studying the differences between article III and the other sections of the ICAC, it is worthwhile to present a summary of its provisions. The article contains twelve paragraphs, five of which are related directly to the conduct or responsibilities of "public officials," a term defined in article I of the convention.

The five aforementioned paragraphs request the issuance of "Standards of conduct for the correct, honorable, and proper fulfillment of public functions," which were also previously defined in this ICAC. These standards are intended to "prevent conflicts of interest and mandate the proper conservation and use of resources entrusted to government officials in the performance of their functions." Paragraph 2 warns that such standards are generally not going to be fulfilled automatically and therefore require "mechanisms to enforce these standards of conduct." To ensure that officials know what is being asked of them in these standards, paragraph 3 requires that the state party provide "Instruction to government personnel to ensure proper understanding of their responsibilities and the ethical standards governing their activities." In another effort to increase the people's trust in the probity of public officials, paragraph 4 requests "systems for registering the earnings, property and liabilities" of public officials and even, "where appropriate, for making such registrations public." To protect public officials who perform their duty of denouncing acts of corruption in good faith, paragraph 8 calls for systems to protect those employees as well as private citizens.

In addition to these five specific sections, the other parts of the article naturally touch upon the consequences for public-sector employees, even though they may not be as direct, as well as the consequences for officials who, as mere citizens, have an administrative relationship with their government. For example, paragraph 5 requests "systems of government hiring and procurement of goods and services that assure the openness, equity and efficiency of such systems," and paragraph 6 focuses on "government revenue collection and control systems that deter corruption."

To conclude the summary, we briefly mention paragraphs 7 and 10, which correspond, respectively, to systems to eliminate tax benefits to entities that make payments for corrupt purposes, and to measures that deter the bribery of national and foreign officials. To strengthen the state's legal status in the combat against domestic corruption, paragraph 9 requires "oversight bodies" but assumes that the government alone cannot eradicate corruption. For that reason, paragraph 11 requires "mechanisms to encourage participation by civil society and non-governmental organizations" in the struggle.

Finally, paragraph 12 confronts the problem of "the relationship between equitable compensation and probity in public service."

Origins

It is impossible to accurately determine the origins of article III. But we do know, at least, that the representatives of Colombia and the United States came to the first meeting of the Organization of American States Working Group in November 1995 with the intent that the convention would contain something more than a few paragraphs on preventing acts of corruption abroad and the strengthening of extradition laws.

The Colombian delegation introduced a draft entitled "Preventive measures," and the United States delegation contributed a preliminary document on principles for public-sector employees. Both reflected an idea that, in the end, the entire group accepted: The ICAC afforded an unprecedented opportunity to fight corruption within a very wide context, not only in its criminal aspects, as relates to the offenses of fraud and the suborning of bankers, but also in daily corruption. In this way, it would take on the challenge of the Summit of the Americas to support efforts favoring probity in government, and be able to tell civil society that the time had come to seriously fight a scourge that was undermining the fight for democracy and free markets.

The Colombian and U.S. proposals were easily combined, as they included ideas supported in laws and standards recently established in those countries. For example, in 1990 the Colombian legislature had approved a broad law requiring probity by public employees against corruption, and in 1993 a new and extensive code of conduct had been implemented for the U.S. executive branch.

It was then deemed appropriate to suggest that the Working Group include among its proposals a draft on preventive measures that would focus on the conduct of public-sector employees while at the same time covering the role of civil society and the private sector.

After submitting each draft to the Working Group, with the Colombian and U.S. proposals, the content grew through suggestions from other countries, until it resulted in the draft transcribed above.

Differences between Article III and the Rest of the Convention

It would appear clear from the beginning that these preventive measures were different from other parts of the document being developed in the Working Group's numerous meetings and discussions, held during its 1995 and 1996 sessions. An examination of those differences, which were briefly explained above, will afford a better understanding of the convention's scope.

Prevention, Not Merely Punishment

The title itself, "Preventive Measures," reflects the first distinction. We might recall that the first item on which attention was focused when preparing the ICAC was the Inter-American Juridical Committee's concern for extradition clauses, restricted to criminal acts, which is important but applicable to a rather limited group, i.e., to those convicted or formally accused of an offense.

Even if it is assumed that fear of being accused of and punished for serious offenses has an impact on preventing acts of corruption, there is also an understanding of the need to prevent corruption through wider resources, of greater scope, than punishment for serious offenses.

Despite the existence of many cultural, historical, and legal differences between the states, there was consistency with respect to the high cost of depending exclusively on criminal punishment for offenses of corruption, a dependence that is also inefficient. It was for this reason that the measures were linked to standards of conduct for public officials and transparency in government, as an important supplement to other provisions of a convention in the course of development.

Less Restrictive, But Very Broad

Although several articles require that the states parties adopt specific actions, such as incorporating certain laws, article III merely states that "the States Parties agree to consider the applicability of measures within their own institutional systems to create, maintain and strengthen" certain mechanisms, systems, and laws. Among other things, the specific nature of the measures would require that each state party take them into account and develop them in accordance with its own customs and institutions, and this was taken into consideration by the article. This may be seen upon examining each measure in article III, such as the standards of conduct for public officials and the role of civil society in the fight against corruption.

At the same time, although article III is less imperative, the range of its coverage is significant, since in each country many people must weigh in on an article's merit and the appropriateness of implementing it. This may be the case, for example, with paragraph five's recognition of the importance of openness in the state's acquisition of property and services, which will serve as a principle for the business sector, commercial corporations, and even the press.

Administrative as Well as Penal

Despite the initial focus on criminal measures such as extradition and the description of various activities, it was always understood that such measures, on their own, would never be capable of winning the fight against corruption.

Criminal proceedings, because they are expensive, because of their long execution time, because they do not apply to many daily acts of corruption, and for other reasons, had to be expanded through administrative measures of the type presented in article III. Such measures, like standards of conduct for public officials and standards for contracting, may strengthen probity in the state sector and increase the people's confidence without involving the criminal system and its complex machinery. In this regard, article III adds a useful element to a convention that has a great deal to do with criminal aspects.

The Role of Civil Society and Nongovernmental Organizations

From a certain standpoint, the most distinctive note of article III may be its reference to civil society and nongovernmental organizations. There is no doubt as to the fact that it is impossible for governments to carry out the fight against corruption without the support of the population itself.

As previously noted, a massive education campaign is necessary to change the attitude that allows corruption to flourish. Paragraph 11 of the article anticipates that the states parties will expect such support and serves as an invitation or, better said, a challenge to civil society and to nongovernmental organizations to participate in that fight. Of course, one of the roles to be played by nongovernmental organizations may be that of monitoring the means by which a state party ratifies and implements the convention and on how the private sector and commercial corporations fulfill their responsibilities with respect to the ICAC.

Government Transparency and Lack of Accountability

Finally, this article is distinguished from other sections of the convention because it promotes one of the instruments universally considered as key in the fight against corruption: government transparency. Almost every paragraph refers to the responsibility of the government and the organizations that do business with the state to provide information that may be used to monitor government activities.

Not only is transparency called for in state processes; it is also requested of public officials. For example, paragraph 4 requires consideration of an earnings declaration system for state employees. Of all the paragraphs of article III, this is perhaps the one that caused the most debate, particularly regarding the need for publishing such declarations. In some countries, this type of declaration is considered as being an invasion of the employee's privacy, even without publication, and possibly as information that might be used for a kidnapping or other harm to the property owner. However, the recommendation was included because of its importance, and it was left to each country to decide on the authority for application and reporting.

This paragraph shows another aspect of the effort to combat corruption: lack of accountability.

Wherever corruption is the topic of discussion, impunity is mentioned, a term used to say that the law does not apply to leaders; that is, certain officials are above the law. The intent of the paragraph on declarations, as well as of other paragraphs of article III—including standards of conduct and mechanisms to enforce those standards—is to end impunity, which many see as a very significant cause of the perpetuation of corruption.

Paragraph-by-Paragraph Analysis and Commentary

We now perform an analysis of each paragraph of article III, in numerical order. As noted above, paragraphs may be grouped by topic, but we hope that the references in the analysis will provide the necessary useful links between them.

It is already known that article III contains the following nonbinding introduction: "For the purposes set forth in Article II of this Convention, the States Parties agree to consider the applicability of measures within their own institutional systems to create, maintain and strengthen" the twelve measures presented therein.

We know that several countries already had laws or regulations, in one form or another, related to those clauses, but in other countries such standards were absent.

It is hoped that in countries where it was not necessary to create that type of a standard, the ICAC will contribute to maintaining and strengthening those that already exist.

Standards of Conduct

"Standards of conduct for the correct, honorable, and proper fulfillment of public functions. These standards shall be intended to prevent conflicts of interest and mandate the proper conservation and use of resources entrusted to government officials in the performance of their functions.

"These standards shall also establish measures and systems requiring government officials to report to appropriate authorities acts of corruption in the performance of public functions.

"Such measures should help preserve the public's confidence in the integrity of public servants and government processes."

The idea of including standards of conduct for public officials within the ICAC originated in the Summit of the Americas Plan of Action. Paragraph 5 requires rules for cases of conflict of interest among officials. The need for such standards of conduct, which appeared first as part of article IX, was introduced early in the Working Group's deliberations as developed by the representatives of Colombia and the United States.

The idea that began as "basic principles" was changed to "preventive measures," in response to comments that held that it would not be appropriate to present principles in a convention of this kind. For that reason, principles became specific measures for implementation, beginning with the need to create standards of conduct, not only to prevent conflicts of interest but also to strengthen protection of the public patrimony and state property by requiring the proper use of property managed by government employees.

Enforcement of Standards of Conduct

"Mechanisms to enforce these standards of conduct."

Although there was little discussion on this paragraph, there was no doubt as to the need to avoid what was referred to as "pious words," an allusion to the situation of several countries that already had laws and rules against corruption, but which were not enforced. The specific mechanisms for enforcing the standards were not mentioned, but it may be undoubtedly assumed that they include mechanisms for the administrative punishment of employees who violate the standards, as well as the possibility of those employees exercising their right of defense vis-à-vis individuals who evaluate their conduct.

Training of Public Officials

In another effort to avoid promulgating ineffective standards of conduct, the need to ensure that public officials receive training, and communications on such standards, was introduced without objection.

We can imagine that the challenge of training the personnel of public entities would include the use of modern communications media, such as television, video, and appropriate publications. In no country would it be logical to assume that state personnel would understand the meaning of "the correct, honorable, and proper fulfillment of public functions," particularly if it were necessary to change the attitudes of those personnel with respect to their duties and tasks. The existence of such standards and citizens' awareness of training programs will also increase their confidence in government probity, or at least in the government's efforts to reduce corruption.

Earnings Declarations

"Systems for registering the earnings, property and liabilities of persons who perform public functions in certain posts as specified by law and, where appropriate, for making such registrations public."

This paragraph caused more debate among the delegations than any other. Although there was awareness of the importance of such declarations, to avoid conflicts of interest and thus reduce opportunities for corruption, there were some fears or doubts regarding this measure, its importance, and its effectiveness for increasing the people's confidence in government probity.

Most particularly, not only with respect to this mechanism but also to various others that had been suggested, there was some fear as to the possibility of this tool against corruption being turned into a weapon against political enemies. This would occur if an accusation of corruption were used as a personal attack rather than as an instrument to improve the implementation and fulfillment of public processes.

Second, there was some concern as to the likely invasion of personal privacy of candidates or state officials. It is always possible that individuals of good character and exceptional reputation might object to the need to declare their property, and consequently expose to the entire world not only the property they own but also that owned by members of their family.

Third, doubts were raised as to the need to disclose information to individuals other than auditors or other officials who require such information to fulfill their obligation to monitor events relating to conflicts of interest, etc., before the occurrence of such a conflict.

There were also differences of opinion regarding the categories of public official who would be required to declare their property. It might be asked, for example, whether requests for declarations by all public employees is a waste of time and a means of trivializing a useful program.

For this reason, as an example of the level of compromise characterizing any agreement of this nature, the final paragraph left to each state party the decision as to the scope of the required declarations and publication.

It would seem obvious that there would be differences in the experiences of the various countries with respect to declarations. For example, in the United States there has been a system to request such declarations of candidates being appointed to any high position of the executive branch of the federal government, including the president and vice president, ever since the Ethics in Government Act of 1978. Such declarations, which are accessible to the public free of charge, must be submitted not only by the candidates, but also by officials, every year and within thirty days after stepping down from a position created by law. These types of declaration are used basically to prevent conflicts between the public official's activities and his economic interests. On several occasions, too, they have prevented involuntary conflicts. This occurs through the intervention of White House officials responsible for monitoring the declarations of presidential appointees, or for the case of employees of an agency, through the efforts of the Office of Government Ethics, an agency created by the act of 1978, which has broad authority in the area of executive branch conduct.

These declarations in the United States cannot be mentioned without noting the interest of the press in having access to them, as well as oversight offices, such as inspectors general, who use them regularly.

The press is always interested in publishing news on the property of senior officials and their spouses, whose property is also included in the declarations, and there is no difficulty identifying the wealthiest individuals in the cabinet, because several newspapers publish that information annually, in May, shortly after the deadline for submitting the property and expenditure declarations.

Oversight officials such as inspectors general use the declarations to establish key facts in their investigations regarding conflicts of interest and other offenses.

In other countries, declarations are submitted in sealed envelopes and only the legal authorities may see them, in the event of an accusation against the declarant.

It is worth noting that a system of declarations, like other preventive measures, can be based on statute or ordered in an executive decree. In some countries, when established only by decree, they may lack sufficient support for their enforcement. By contrast, systems established by statute may take too long before they enter into force.

It is therefore the states parties who must make the decision to address the challenge of the convention, not only with respect to article III, but for the other sections as well.

Transparency in Government Contracting

"Systems of government hiring and procurement of goods and services that assure the openness, equity and efficiency of such systems."

As early a document as the Declaration by the Summit of the Americas noted the importance of government transparency as a guarantee of democracy and proper administration.

To this end, preventive measures focus on the government's need to provide information to the people, not only when this information is required, but also in advance, on all areas most susceptible to corruption. For that reason, this paragraph has two key aspects: the hiring of public officials and the procurement of goods and services by the state.

Undoubtedly, when the average citizen thinks about corruption in the public sector, these two aspects of government activity come immediately to mind.

The openness mentioned in this paragraph would be effective for increasing competition and improving prices in public purchasing and increasing the quality of candidates for positions. For reasons of fairness, this system must be complemented by mechanisms to appeal unfair decisions.

Efficiency would also result from competition in those systems, which have so much to do with the ways citizens measure probity in the public sector.

The United States has various laws aimed at ensuring transparency in government acts. The Freedom of Information Act requires various agencies to provide any citizen who so requests any government documents not excepted for reasons of security, intelligence, or any cause legally established beforehand, without need to provide a reason. If the document is refused, the citizen may resort to the courts to obtain an order for it to be issued. The Privacy Act establishes a similar mechanism, in favor of the directly interested citizens, for record data mentioning an individual. The Government Sunshine Act allows private citizens to attend any deliberation of the collegiate bodies of the executive branch, such as committees that oversee the functioning of public services.

Other administrative procedural rules require that the government submit for public consideration plans for the legal regulation of specific matters that would affect the life of the community, as well as to listen to and respond to suggestions received from the people. This includes mechanisms requiring that public agencies state their reasons for procuring specific goods or services and the methods that they will use in doing so. There are also laws relating to consultative committees, making it possible for various interested sectors to participate in government advising on the development of specific legal standards, and those advisory groups must have a balanced membership.

Special Revenue Collection and Control Systems

"Government revenue collection and control systems that deter corruption."

This paragraph was the result of several suggestions on the need to protect state revenue, because revenue locations, such as customs offices and other facilities at which funds are received, are vulnerable to corruption.

At these locations, corrupt public servants not only find opportunities for theft but also the ability to give preferences and accept bribes to avoid applying laws and rules relating to the payment of fines, fees, and other debts to the state.

This section, like others in article III, reflects recognition of the state's ability to reduce corruption by increasing the efficiency of its procedures—through the use of computers, for example—in at least two senses. First, with increased efficiency in fulfilling the state processes, the public should find it less necessary to pay bribes to receive the expected services. Second, by using computers and other modern accounting mechanisms, it should be more difficult for public officials to engage in abuse when performing their work; for example, by maintaining the state patrimony and using state property for unauthorized purposes.

Elimination of Favorable Tax Treatment to Those Who Engage in Corrupt Acts

"Laws that refuse favorable tax treatment for any individual or corporation for expenditures made in violation of the anticorruption laws of the States Parties."

As we noted earlier, one goal of several states parties, the United States in particular, was for the convention to classify acts of corruption abroad, i.e., the offering of bribes to public officials of another country to perform official services.

In certain countries, such acts, in addition to not being an offense, may even be considered as constituting necessary business expenses, and therefore receive favorable tax treatment.

The purpose of paragraph 7, together with that of article VIII, is to eliminate transnational bribery.

Protection of Those Who Report Acts of Corruption

"Systems for protecting public servants and private citizens who, in good faith, report acts of corruption, including protection of their identities, in accordance with their Constitutions and the basic principles of their domestic legal systems."

Some negotiators set forth arguments in favor of the need for public officials and private citizens as sources to report acts of corruption.

Undoubtedly, individuals who report such acts, particularly in the case of public servants, run a certain risk of reprisal and deserve government protection from any harm they may suffer in fulfilling their official duties. However, as we noted in the comments to section 4, reasonable weapons for fighting corruption may also be used against political enemies. For that reason, negotiators included the words "in good faith" to prevent abuse of the protection suggested in this paragraph. Such a protection system may include, as in United States, an oversight body with authority, for example, to prohibit an agency at which a whistleblower is employed from taking action against him until after an investigation of the report has been carried out.

In the United States, the office responsible for offering such protection is called the Office of the Special Counsel, and its head is appointed by the president and approved by the Senate. He operates independently of the heads of all other agencies and departments in the executive branch.

Oversight Bodies

"Oversight bodies with a view to implementing modern mechanisms for preventing, detecting, punishing and eradicating corrupt acts."

There was not much discussion on this section, probably because there was no doubt as to the need for such bodies, but also because a convention should not include many details, such as examples of specific bodies. Certainly, it was hoped that in implementing the ICAC, particularly with regard to the fulfillment of article XIV—assistance and cooperation—there would be a great deal of information exchanged between the states parties on their experiences with oversight bodies. Of course, in several countries there already were certain oversight bodies, such as attorneys general, auditors, and financial and auditing managers. But the new focus on modern mechanisms, which was emphasized at the beginning, pointed to the need to consider new preventive measures, in addition to greater efficiency in those already existing. These might include, for example, ethics offices for training public employees, offices to protect those making reports in good faith, offices to analyze property and earnings declarations, etc. Since corruption uses modern methods to commit crimes, society must also adopt modern mechanisms to defend itself against this threat.

Measures to Deter Domestic and Foreign Bribery

"Deterrents to the bribery of domestic and foreign government officials, such as mechanisms to ensure that publicly held companies and other types of associations maintain books and records which, in reasonable detail, accurately reflect the acquisition and disposition of property, and have sufficient domestic accounting controls to enable their officers to detect corrupt acts."

As the most active proponent against foreign acts of corruption, the U.S. delegation introduced this paragraph as the result of its experience to date with applying the Foreign Corrupt Practices Act of 1977. In addition to the criminal sections, the act contains certain requirements relating to methods that large companies must use to maintain their domestic accounts.

Consequently, heads of organizations most likely to commit acts of bribery abroad have no way of avoiding their responsibility by claiming ignorance with respect to domestic or foreign acts of bribery.

It remains to be seen how the other states parties will develop such measures, not only to reduce corruption within their own agencies, but to fulfill article VII as well, on transnational bribery.

The importance of sections such as this, which emphasize the private sector's role in the fight against corruption, cannot be overestimated. It cannot be assumed that without bribery originating from the business sector there is no corruption, since this scourge primarily involves the behavior of public officials. Nevertheless, this type of bribery plays a significant role in perpetuating corruption. The enforcement of section 10 can do much to reduce it.

Encouraging Participation by Civil Society

"Mechanisms to encourage participation by civil society and non-governmental organizations in efforts to prevent corruption."

Undoubtedly, negotiators noted that a fight against corruption would need to have not only the support but also the participation of the people.

The role of commercial corporations and the private sector in the survival of corruption has already been mentioned.

Because it is a social phenomenon that, in certain countries, constitutes the rule rather than the exception, it was necessary to involve civil society and nongovernmental organizations in the fight against corruption.

The negotiators wasted no time defining civil society or describing non-governmental organizations in any state party. Nor was this necessary, since as a result of the Summit of the Americas and other well-publicized efforts in several countries of the hemisphere, the issue of corruption had already received more attention than ever in the press and in the creation of organizations such as Transparency International.

The same applies to other measures of article III, in that the drafters did not enter into detail, but recognized a consensus as to the opportunities that would arise, after ratifying the convention, to share information on methods of implementation within each state party, including experience in encouraging participation as mentioned here.

One aspect of participation by civil society will of course be the dissemination of information in schools and all environments as to the importance of government probity and the right of citizens to know how the government is meeting its responsibilities.

As has been noted, the task of generating awareness among the population regarding the existence and seriousness of the problem of corruption would have to be accepted by civil society and nongovernmental organizations.

Study of Other Measures to Prevent Corruption

The negotiators dedicated a great deal of attention to the issue of a possible definition of corruption, but decided not to offer one. Article VI describes several examples of behavior considered as being corrupt, but almost no attention was paid to the causes of the corruption. However, several negotiators, including the authors of this book, had participated in the First World Conference on Ethics in Government, which took place in Washington in November 1994. At that conference—and surely in others that had been held before and after the Summit of the Americas—the need to better understand the causes of corruption was discussed.

At the Washington conference, the relationship between corruption and compensation of public officials received a great deal of attention, particularly from participants from developing countries, who noted very significant differences from the situation in the United States. In many countries government wages are not expected to be sufficient to put food on the table and a roof over the heads of many public employees, particularly those at the very bottom of the compensation structure.

For that reason, and/or other reasons having to do with issues such as accountability and the scarcity of studies and literature on the causes and results of corruption, it was felt to be very appropriate and important that the convention recognize the need to perform more studies and research on the issue.

Certainly, much of the legislation and regulation that the ICAC was requesting to obtain the expected results would have to be based on up-to-date information and new underlying trends. For that reason, the first draft included a paragraph that called for "the study of other preventive measures, including the relationship between fair compensation and probity in the public service." No negotiator objected to this paragraph, as it was suggested.

In fact, this paragraph was taken from the final negotiations in Washington to the Caracas meeting in March 1996. However, for reasons no one has been able to explain to date, the final version of the convention, in its paragraph 12 on studies, refers only to the issue of fair wages. There is no doubt as to the importance of this issue, but we hope that no one thinks it is the only relevant issue in the fight against corruption that deserves serious study. For example, some studies that show how corruption threatens the population by reducing opportunities for food, medicine, etc., which the government is responsible for providing to people, may convince citizens of the need to not participate further in acts of corruption.

Conclusion

It is clear that the convention in general and article III in particular reflect an unprecedented official admission and social challenge. This admission by the governments of the hemisphere as to the existence of corruption as a powerful threat to the development of democracy and the free market must not be considered as being an issue of low importance.

Over the last few years, it has ceased to be impossible to speak openly of corruption, from the highest government offices to meetings of nongovernmental organizations.

The ICAC is a clear and official declaration that the time has come to use all available instruments, in all sectors of society, in that fight.

Article III provides some specific suggestions for each state party to consider. It also challenges civil society to become involved and to monitor the government's compliance with its commitments under the convention.

There is no serious discussion of the issue of corruption that does not refer to three indispensable factors of success in the fight against that evil; or better said, in the fight to increase probity in public affairs, which involves eliminating impunity, increasing transparency in government administration, and promoting active participation by educated citizens.

The convention and article III are an efficient framework for those three concepts. It remains to be seen, now, whether we will take advantage of this opportunity, this window that must not be closed, by failing to take appropriate action. We must also determine whether the Organization of American

States' ambitious plans for implementing the ICAC are as successful as its development work.

There still remain sections of the convention that must await the publication of complicated laws by the legislatures of the member countries, and implementation by legal structures that are currently weak.

Article III, with its focus on preventive measures, offers a platform on which all sectors of Inter-American society have an important role. The world will be watching the outcome.

ARTICLE IV

SCOPE

This Convention is applicable provided that the alleged act of corruption has been committed or has effects in a State Party.

General Information

The word "scope" refers to the physical background on which the convention is required to operate. In this case, this physical background is that of the states parties; that is, that of the states that signed the document, either because, as the article notes, an act of corruption has been committed in one of the states parties, or it has effects in one of the states parties.

This article, the draft of which was approved without too much discussion, is fundamentally important in international documents such as the one being analyzed.

The interpretation as to the scope of this standard will define the application or exclusion of the convention in doubtful cases.

However, the definition of scope is incomplete, since if the article in question is taken in isolation, the convention appears limited to the consequences of an act of corruption that has already been committed, since the clause reads, "provided that the alleged act of corruption has been committed or has effects." According to these terms, the article appears exclusively oriented toward jurisdiction, extradition, assistance, and cooperation in measures relating to property. But these measures, aimed at increasing the efficiency of prosecuting offenses assumed to have been committed, represent only half the convention, with regard to either the volume or the importance of the issues. The other half is represented by the states' obligation to legislate specific matters and the commitment to consider including certain penal or administrative measures in their respective laws. The convention also applies to these commitments.

Application Principles

According to the article in question, the convention applies whenever an act of corruption is committed on the territory of a state party or has effects in a state party.

When we speak of "scope," regulations are always based on "territory," which continues to be the point of reference even in cases where a principle other than territoriality applies.

The article may therefore be divided into two parts, both of which define principles very familiar to those conversant in the field of criminal law: the principle of territoriality and the principle of defense.

In criminal matters, the principle of territoriality implies that a state tries all offenses committed on its territory. The principle of defense means that a state may prosecute offenses committed outside its territory but whose effects occurred on its territory.

Criminal law recognizes a third principle: that of legal status or nationality, to which we refer in the comments to article V. But, in all cases, application of this principle will require that the offense, participation in committing it, or its concealment be committed or take effect in a state party and that it be another state party that files the complaint.

ARTICLE V

JURISDICTION

1. *Each State Party shall adopt such measures as may be necessary to es-tablish its jurisdiction over the offenses it has established in accordance with this Convention when the offense in question is committed in its territory.*
2. *Each State Party may adopt such measures as may be necessary to establish its jurisdiction over the offenses it has established in accordance with this Convention when the offense is committed by one of its nationals or by a person who habitually resides in its territory.*
3. *Each State Party shall adopt such measures as may be necessary to establish its jurisdiction over the offenses it has established in accordance with this Convention when the alleged criminal is present in its territory and it does not extradite such person to another country on the ground of the nationality of the alleged criminal.*
4. *This Convention does not preclude the application of any other rule of criminal jurisdiction established by a State Party under its domestic law.*

General Information

The point of this article goes to the very heart of the convention. As may be seen, it seeks to force the states to prosecute crimes of corruption; a scope that would have been inadmissible not too many years ago, under the pretext of nonintervention in the domestic affairs of another state. But we have already noted, in the introduction to this work and in the comments to the preamble, the new stage being opened in the world when the international community becomes aware of the need to engage the states beyond their borders, in certain areas whose treatment is too sensitive to governments as to be excluded from the interest of the international community. Such was the case of human rights, the environment, and now, corruption.

The article on jurisdiction is closely related to article IV, as to the scope of application, but—as may be easily seen—the articles do not have the same coverage.

The scope of application addresses the physical background on which the entire convention is based, in all its parts, including jurisdiction, as well as assistance and cooperation, extradition, measures relating to property, etc., and—although this is not expressed in article IV—the obligation to legislate (see the final paragraph of "General Information" in the comments to article IV).

Principle of Territoriality

The first part of article V appears not to require too much analysis. Provided that the act of corruption was committed on the territory of a state party, the convention applies. However, this raises a question: what is the scope of the phrase: "has been committed"? Of course, there is no doubt when the act has been initiated and carried out entirely on a territory, including—as the case may be—the actions of the participants and instigators. But what happens when the course of the corrupt act extends across several states, some of which may not be party to the convention?

The convention must apply in any case where the criminal action or a portion thereof takes place in some state party, even if it involves a secondary participant or instigator. This statement is independent of the decision regarding the articles of the convention that must be applied. For example, extradition may not be appropriate, but assistance and cooperation may well be. But the convention applies.

Principle of Legal Status or Nationality

The principle of legal status or nationality is not as widely used in the world as that of territoriality. It must be clarified that when this principle is mentioned here, it refers to "legal status of the active party," that is, taking into consideration the nationality of the instigator of the offense rather than that of the victim.

In general, the principle of legal status consists in the possibility or even obligation of a state to punish its nationals for offenses committed anywhere on the planet, and today perhaps we should also say even off the planet.

Certainly, the implementation of such a principle by some states creates conflicts when it clashes with the application by others of the principle of territoriality. This is the classic case of an offense committed by a national of one country that follows the principle of nationality on the territory of another that follows exclusively the principle of territoriality. Both states will attempt to exercise their jurisdiction simultaneously. Of course, the conflict is resolved according to bilateral or multilateral treaties; but in mere theory, the opposition exists.

It was precisely the lack of agreement on the principle of legal status that was the reason for the optional form of section 2 of article V: "Each State Party may adopt such measures as may be necessary to establish its jurisdiction . . . when the offense is committed by one of its nationals or by a person who habitually resides in its territory."

Regarding this form, one might very well question the value of a clause written to be optional, such that the state party may or may not exercise its jurisdiction.

The following response could be given to an objection of this kind:

1. Many times, moral principles are introduced into the text of documents that, now more than ever, under the watchful eyes of an attentive and informed international community, a state cannot fail to enforce without incurring a political cost.
2. In any case, the clause is not harmless from a strictly legal point of view. What is more, it recognizes the states' possibility of applying the principle of legal status for acts of corruption, an authority that is not insignificant when one analyzes the possible domestic and external legal conflicts that may arise. That is, the convention does not state that the principle of territoriality is the only one possible.

Extradition Not Granted

By contrast, the draft of section 3, article V, returns to the binding formula, this time to force a state to exercise its jurisdiction if it does not consent to the extradition of a national.

As may be seen, the situation this clause seeks to avoid is the criminal's lack of accountability. If extradition is not granted because the accused is a national of the country that received the request, then that country is required to try him in accordance with its own laws and courts.

During the negotiations at the OAS, there was a discussion as to whether this clause should be limited to cases of extradition not granted because of the nationality of the accused criminal, or rather be extended to extradition not granted for any reason.

An overview of the reasons for which extradition might generally be denied shows that the state could only be truly required to exercise its jurisdiction if its refusal was in response to the criminal's nationality. If extradition were denied because of the lapse of the alleged offense's statute of limitations, the requested state cannot be asked to try a person for an offense for which the statute of limitations has already expired. With even less reason can it be asked to do so if the alleged offense is not covered by the laws of the requested state. And if extradition is denied because of formal defects in the petition, whether or not those defects can be repaired, it would seem reasonable that, at least in any case, the requested state be required to exercise its jurisdiction in substitution of the defective extradition request. Otherwise, this would be tantamount to requiring that the requested state be more efficient than the interested party itself, not to mention the fact that, on many occasions, the defect in the petition affects the clear understanding of its very essence.

To the Benefit of Jurisdiction

Because the ICAC has at all times sought to favor the exercise of jurisdiction, section 4 stipulates that the "convention does not preclude the application of any other rule of criminal jurisdiction established by a State Party under its domestic law." This provision must be interpreted in this sense.

ARTICLE VI

ACTS OF CORRUPTION

1. This Convention is applicable to the following acts of corruption:

a. The solicitation or acceptance, directly or indirectly, by a government official or a person who performs public functions, of any article of monetary value, or other benefit, such as a gift, favor, promise or advantage for himself or for another person or entity, in exchange for any act or omission in the performance of his public functions;

b. The offering or granting, directly or indirectly, to a government official or a person who performs public functions, of any article of monetary value, or other benefit, such as a gift, favor, promise or advantage for himself or for another person or entity, in exchange for any act or omission in the performance of his public functions;

    c. Any act or omission in the discharge of his duties by a government official or a person who performs public functions for the purpose of illicitly obtaining benefits for himself or for a third party;

    d. The fraudulent use or concealment of property derived from any of the acts referred to in this article;

    e. Participation as a principal, coprincipal, instigator, accomplice or accessory after the fact, or in any other manner, in the commission or attempted commission of, or in any collaboration or conspiracy to commit, any of the acts referred to in this article.

2. This Convention shall also be applicable by mutual agreement between or among two or more States Parties with respect to any other act of corruption not described herein.

General Information

The article in question is the core of the convention, because it defines acts of corruption for purposes of applying the convention's clauses. It does not offer an abstract definition of corruption, which perhaps would have been useful in the preamble, but rather describes, with a clearly practical purpose, the behavior that could trigger application of the convention's mechanisms and commitments, such as the obligation to legislate (i.e., to classify), extradition, assistance and cooperation, precautionary measures, etc.

    Simply put, through this article the states say that, for now, they are bound and required to combat the practices described herein, and to mutually collaborate in doing so. This does not mean that the states parties believed that corruption is completely defined by those acts. Indeed, the very draft of the article makes it clear that corruption is a wider notion, in that it states, "This Convention is applicable to the following acts of corruption." This means that there may be other acts of corruption that have not yet been taken into consideration by the ICAC.

    Article VI describes conduct that the states may indisputably leave to be legislated within their domestic law. To this must be added the conduct described in articles VIII and IX, which have the same force as article VI, for purposes of triggering the convention's mechanisms.

    Another consideration to be made when reading both article VI and articles VIII, IX, and XI corresponds to the terms used in describing the conduct. There will always be a temptation to compare those terms with the ones that the standards of positive law or the legal terminology of each country employ or might employ and to establish differences, which will undoubtedly exist. Nevertheless, it must not be forgotten that these articles do not constitute classifications of criminal law, but rather generic descriptions that point to more accurate definitions of positive law. Indeed, one of the difficulties of an international document consists in the differences of terminology that might exist among the signatory countries. For that reason, the convention attempts to be as specific as possible without going so far that such specificity could be called upon to limit the scope of the commitment.

Passive Bribery

Paragraph a of section 1, article VI, describes two levels of passive bribery as acts of corruption: solicitation and acceptance of a bribe by a public official.

Acceptance corresponds to the bribe itself, and solicitation refers to the attempt, although paragraph e later explicitly covers attempts for all the acts in question. The description emphasizes, however, that accepting money may be the consequence of a bribe not solicited, but granted nevertheless.

With respect to the notion of a public official, i.e., the suborned party, we should go back to the commentary on article I and recall that, for purposes of the convention, this category includes those who have been selected, appointed, or elected to perform activities or functions in the name of the state or in the service of the state, even if they are not yet acting in their position. This is logical, because a deputy who has been elected to a position, even though not yet serving in the parliament, may very likely be suborned, for example, to approve or propose a specific legislative measure upon taking possession of his seat. Something similar may occur with a judge who has been appointed, but not yet taken over his court, who at that stage may be suborned by some interested party to a case filed in the court to which the magistrate will later be assigned.

We believe that the conclusion we have just expressed, combined with the obligation entered into by the states in article VII of the ICAC, demands a change or expansion in the criminal standards of the signatory countries who did not consider this situation.

The passive subject is also included in the phrase "or a person who performs public functions." When the ICAC was drafted, there was not a great deal of consensus regarding the scope of this addendum. Article VIII was also prepared prior to article I on definitions. However, as clearly stated in a subsequent OAS study titled "Adaptation of Peruvian Criminal Law to the Inter-American Convention against Corruption," this phrase must be linked to a distinction that legal writing makes between "public function" and "public official."[2] Certainly, the notion of "public function" has a broader meaning, and there may be individuals who perform public functions without being officials, such as the authorities of certain professional corporations to which the state assigns registration duties, or experts in a legal case, as well as private individuals to whom certain public authorities, in some countries, grant monitoring and enforcement powers that clearly fall to the state, such as vehicle inspection and seizure, for

---

[2] The study was carried out by Dr. Felipe Villavicencio Terreros, in Lima, May 2000.

example. If these individuals are suborned, the performance of a public function is prevented or distorted.

Solicitations or acceptances, as indicated in this section, may be direct or indirect. Requests or acceptance are direct when the public official, personally or through some means of communication, performs them for an individual who will pay a bribe, with no intermediary familiar with the extent of the acts. A request made by mail must be considered as being direct, even though a messenger intervened, since that employee's participation is merely mechanical and he is unaware of the content of the correspondence. If the person serving as the vehicle for the solicitation, on the other hand, knows its content and actively participates in the request, that request is indirect. Insinuations, as well as an attitude on the part of a public official that is intended to demonstrate to a private party that he will not achieve his purpose except through a bribe, also constitute indirect requests.

The object of the bribe is any article of monetary value, or other benefit, such as a gift, favor, promise, or advantage. Unfortunately, the description does not refer expressly to money because, in the first place, it was assumed that the expression "any article of monetary value" was sufficient. And it is true that for a convention, which does not require the precision of a classification of crimes, that phrase is sufficient, but it is technically not the best solution. Also in this case, the style committee did not have a unanimous opinion as to its authority to add the term "money," although, in our judgment, in this case it would have been able to do so.

The description of the object of the bribe includes, certainly, not only pecuniary property but also any other benefit, such as a gift, favor, promise, or advantage. As may be seen, this is a mere description of the phrase "other benefits." This is logical, because a favor unable to be valued in money may represent a greater incentive than a physical good, in certain situations. The same thing applies to promises or advantages, which may or may not have monetary value. Donations, on the other hand, always have monetary value, although in some legal systems they are not linked to the performance or omission of an act and this fact is precisely what distinguishes them from a bribe. But the word was not included in a country's specific technical sense, but rather in its widest sense: as a synonym for gift.

The recipient of the object involved in the bribe need not necessarily be the official, but also "another person or entity" as clearly stated in paragraph a. The official may wish to benefit another person or institution to later receive a favor or recognition, or engage in a specific form of "altruism," and the article makes no distinctions in this sense, because in any case, the public function has been degraded and legal security has been broken.

The purpose of the bribe is to engage in any act or omission in the performance of his public functions.

Such "act" may consist in awarding a bid, signing an agreement, assigning priority to a payment, or hundreds of variables with respect to which the imagination of corrupt officials is always more fruitful than that of the lawmakers. "Omission" may consist in failing to apply a penalty, neglecting to monitor, etc.

It is to be noted that the act or omission need not be illegal to be included among acts of corruption. This is logical, since if the act or omission were not promoted through fulfillment of a duty, but rather by the hope of recompense unrelated to the benefits to which the official is entitled for his work, the government would have been corrupted in any case, because:

1. Justice has been altered, since the official receives recompense for performing an act for which he was already paid by the state. Specifically, in this case, the taxpayer pays double, because he has contributed through his taxes to supporting the wages of the official, and he also paid the bribe.
2. A potential factor of inequality is introduced between administrators, since through bribery, public employees are tempted to assign priority to acts that benefit those who pay them.
3. A deep mistrust in the justice of the act and the virtue of the official, as well as the entire government, is generated.
4. The foundation has been laid for extortion, which many officials engage in when they solicit or allow a bribe to be paid in order to do their duty.

Of course, when the act or omission that is the object of the bribe is illegitimate, the injustice is aggravated, and to a certain extent, the negative social effects are greater. We say "to a certain extent," because a bribe of that kind is an unjust act in itself. But from another point of view, a community that is forced to pay even for recognition of its lawful rights has arrived at a very serious and broad point of injustice. It is widely believed that even in the most corrupt countries, legitimate acts will always be more numerous than illegitimate ones. If the performance of those acts is due to a payment, this will be a sign of the alarming level that corruption has attained in that country.

To be classified as corrupt, an act or omission must be linked to the performance of the employee's public functions. That is the sense of the final part of paragraph a of section 1, article VI: "in the performance of his public functions." This expression must not be interpreted as the period during which the official is present in performing his duties.

Active Bribery

The expressions "active bribery" or "active subornment" refer to the act of offering or granting property or advantages to a public official to achieve a specified act or omission, as described in section 1(b), article VI, "the offering or granting, directly or indirectly."

This universally accepted method of referring to this act introduces a certain level of confusion. The word "active," by its own meaning, appears to refer to conduct more serious than the word "passive." And there are individuals who maintain that, indeed, paying a bribe is a graver moral violation than accepting one. We believe otherwise. A public official is not under any pressure from a private individual to accept a bribe, except in the case of another offense, such as a threat, for example, but that is not the case in question. By contrast, a corrupt public official frequently is the source of pressure to a private party to grant a bribe, through manipulation of bids in government procurement procedures, processing delays, etc. Certainly, the briber and the recipient always have the necessary freedom to not act illegally, but for the official to not accept the bribe, he need merely fulfill his obligation. A private individual, on the other hand, to reject a request for a bribe, must at times bear a severe personal or business loss.

In any case, this is a moral distinction that, as is logical, is not at all reflected in the ICAC, which does not even use the terms "active bribe" and "passive bribe."

As for the rest, the same considerations as made in the preceding paragraph apply to the analysis of paragraph b.

Fraudulent Administration, Incompatible Negotiations, Nonfulfillment of Duties

Paragraph c describes a notion that, depending upon the various laws, may be identified as fraudulent administration, negotiations incompatible with the public function, failure by a public official to fulfill his duties, or other names that might correspond to the quest for illegal benefits from state activities that do not include bribes, in the countries of the hemisphere. This is "any act or omission in the discharge of his duties by a government official or a person who performs public functions for the purpose of illicitly obtaining benefits for himself or for a third party."

As in all cases, the description seeks to be as broad as possible, so as not to exclude classifications of crimes that might exist in the various laws with respect to similar conduct, but at the same time, to commit the signatory countries to adapting their classifications of crimes, and thereby ensure the imposition of penalties for all conduct covered by paragraph c.

We must note the difference between bribery and the act of corruption mentioned in this title. Bribery necessarily includes the delivery of some value or the performance of some favor, to encourage the official to perform the act or omission being sought. By contrast, in the concept described here, no mention is made of any good in exchange, but rather, the official simply performs an act or incurs an omission with the direct intent of benefiting himself or a third party. To be classified as corruption, the description does not require that the third party in question share in the benefits with the official. It does require, however, that the benefit be obtained illegally, as is logical, since if the word "illegally" were not included to qualify the act or the omission, any activity by the official to obtain a benefit would be considered as being an act of corruption. Thus, the very work of employees in exchange for their normal compensation or the current services that agents provide to the benefit of the public would be classified as acts of corruption.

The paragraph does not state that the benefits sought must necessarily be economic. This distinguishes the concept in question from fraudulent administration. Nor does the description mention a lack of compatibility between the aforementioned conduct and the public function, since such a lack of compatibility would appear to be implicit. For that reason, we note that the draft is sufficiently broad as to include various concepts or names under the positive legal systems.

We should point out, once again, that any international document covering criminal law does not, on its own, constitute a classification of crimes. As in this case, it simply seeks to encourage such a classification, as well as to cover the classifications of crimes already existing in the states parties, to allow assistance, cooperation, and extradition when acts coinciding with the description in the commitment are noted.

Asset Laundering

Paragraph d includes among corrupt acts "the fraudulent use or concealment of property" deriving from such acts.

In sum, this paragraph describes concealment, the laundering of money or property in general, which in one case may take the form of fraudulent use of property and, in another, simple concealment.

When we speak of use, the reference is obviously to an individual other than the instigator of the offense, since use by the instigator is generally included within the definition of the offense itself and therefore does not constitute a different act of corruption.

Note that this paragraph, when referring to use, adds the term "fraudulent."

That is to say, the use of property originating from an offense against the government, for one's own benefit, can only be considered as being an act of corruption under the convention (or a new offense, under the law of the states) when there is knowledge of its source.

To completely exhaust the analysis, it would be necessary to determine whether potential fraud is also sufficient to classify use as a corrupt act. In other words, it must be determined whether this conduct is a corrupt act when the party using the property has, or should reasonably have, suspicions as to its origin but his acts or omissions are indicative of indifference with regard to such uncertainty.

In such a case, we believe that the old Roman legal principle must be applied: "Ubi lex non distinguere, nec non distinguere habemus" (where the law makes no distinctions, neither must we make distinctions). In the end, potential fraud is fraud. The convention does distinguish between direct, indirect, or potential fraud, such that potential fraud relating to the use of property is sufficient for that use to be considered as being a corrupt act.

This is also the most reasonable solution and the one most appropriate for a criminal policy that truly seeks to be effective. There are numerous circumstances in which the context, given the legal status of the individual involved in the use, indicates that he could not have been unaware of the origin of the property, even if he had no proof or direct information relating to the offense.

With respect to "concealment," the convention does not even require fraud for that conduct to be considered as being a corrupt act. In principle, and in accordance with this draft, blame or negligence is used to include concealment among corrupt acts. We believe, however, that it must be a case of gross negligence, i.e., conduct that anticipated or reasonably should have anticipated the possibility of the illegal event, even if hopeful doubt remains as to the absence of any illegality. In the item in question, there is only a very subtle and subjective distinction between gross negligence and potential fraud.

We believe that this category cannot include acts based on an absolute failure to represent the illicit origins of the property, depending upon the circumstances of the case, unless the instigator of the concealment was legally required to take certain measures or precautions that he did not take to identify such origins.

This paragraph of article VI is particularly important for the purposes of the ICAC. Laundering is the axis of one of the principal lines of combat against corruption, drug trafficking, and organized crime. Discouraging conduct of this nature is also a very efficient action to prevent the crime.

We will refer further to laundering in our comments on the paragraph on concealment.

Instigation, Participation, Concealment, and Other Concepts

Paragraph e of section 1, article VI, drafted in accordance with a proposal from the Jamaican delegation, provides an exhaustive description of other forms of participation and again includes concealment.

This paragraph describes as a corrupt act the "participation as a principal, coprincipal, instigator, accomplice or accessory after the fact, or in any other manner, in the commission or attempted commission or in any collaboration or conspiracy to commit" the corrupt acts the article previously defined.

The word "participation" is used in the grammatical sense of the term, rather than in the technical-criminal meaning of the word. In its technical sense, participation includes "complicity" and "instigation" as an accessory form. But the paragraph in question introduces a list of all forms of relationship to an offense: principal, coprincipal, instigator, complicity, concealment, attempt, collaboration in the offense, etc.

The inclusion of principal and coprincipal was unnecessary in the paragraph, because they are implied in the list of corrupt acts contained in paragraphs a, b, and c of section 1, article VI. Their inclusion acts as a legal reinforcement of such concepts.

Instigation, within the context of offenses of corruption, is extremely important. In many instances, instigators of a bribe have greater moral responsibility than the actual principal himself. Let us imagine, for example, the legal adviser of a company who encourages one of the company's employees to give a bribe to resolve a case.

From the standpoint of government, there may be political officials, for example, who instigate staff employees to illegitimately benefit a company that has contributed in some electoral campaign. The instigators are often the most important agents of corruption.

An accomplice or participant is an individual who consciously cooperates with the criminal activity. He may be a primary participant, without whose intervention the offense cannot be carried out, or a secondary participant, who assists in committing the offense, but whose cooperation is not a determining factor in the success of the illegal proceeding.

We have already mentioned concealment in the commentary to the paragraph on asset laundering.

We noted that attacking this concept is a fundamental tool in the fight against corruption.

Concealment may take on numerous forms. One of them, which does not represent a technically distinct category, but which common language has distinguished, is that of laundering, to which we just referred. Corrupt officials generally must conceal property obtained through ill-gotten money, or show the property but conceal its true origin.

Property may be concealed through intermediate parties who in some places are known as "straw men." They appear to be the true owners of the property the official acquires with the proceeds of the offense. At the same time, corrupt officials, who do not always have a great number of people they completely trust for these purposes, tend to require their accessories after the fact to provide "a counterdocument" to ensure the return of the property to their ownership, after the lapse of a significant period of time from the date they left public office. These counterdocuments take the form of promises of sale or donation, with the date left blank, which the accessories after the fact issue in favor of the officials who delivered the property to them. This situation is difficult, but not impossible to remedy.

Many countries register asset declarations of public officials and their direct family members, through which oversight authorities may examine changes in the property of officials and compare those changes with their lawful earnings, both within and outside the government. Sometimes these records are public; that is, they may be consulted by any citizen.

Despite the existence of this useful tool, concealment, through simulated owners who are not the direct family members to whom we just referred, continues to be a problem. We believe that to reduce the likelihood of this unfortunately effective tool of corruption, to the extent that national constitutions so permit, the states may promulgate laws that render invalid or, at least, non-binding or unenforceable by the courts, all promises of sale, donation, or irrevocable sale mandate not registered by officials in their asset records or included on their declarations, within a certain period of time after they take office or on the date of those instruments. The states thereby expose corrupt officials to the possibility of betrayal by their own accessories after the fact, who could thereby close out the counterdocument and sell the ill-gotten property.

No one imagines that these remedies could be a solution in all cases, but no method that contributes to reducing the likelihood of corruption should be discarded.

Another well-known procedure for concealing illegitimate money is secret accounts, basically in countries with a deep tradition of respect for bank secrecy. We cannot classify the action of banks as "concealment." We refer to this matter in the commentary to article XVI.

By contrast with concealment carried out for purposes of corrupt acts, which generally consist in concealing property obtained illegally, laundering is a form of concealment that seeks to disguise the source of the money, such that, after its origin has been "cleaned," the official may be perfectly confident in using the money in broad daylight. Companies tend to be created for this purpose, whether profitable or not, whose officers are listed as owners, perhaps from a time prior to their taking office; these are always difficult to monitor for accounting purposes. Such companies declare earnings higher than they really are, because in actuality, these false earnings consist precisely of concealed money obtained through acts of corruption in the public function.

Monitoring this situation is difficult for three reasons:

1. States, in most cases, are prepared to monitor tax evasion, but for obvious tax reasons, they are reluctant to investigate whether companies declare excess earnings.

2. "Launderers" tend to use companies whose earnings are very difficult to monitor, whether because their customers are not identifiable, or at least do not appear on invoices or payment receipts, or because such receipts do not exist because of the rapid selling conditions required by the activities of that kind of company. We will not mention examples of activities of this kind so as not to implicate the thousands of companies that engage in such activities lawfully, as well as because of the large number of commercial methods likely to be used for laundering, which is currently one of the international community' greatest concerns.

3. Technology and the speed of communications allow money to circulate through a large number of destinations, within a very short period of time.

In all cases, for concealment to be considered as such, there must be no prior promise from the instigator of the offense to the accessory after the fact, since if there were such a promise, the concealment would become participation, i.e., complicity.

Furthermore, despite what was mentioned above with respect to concealment directed toward effects, it must be clear that to be considered as such, it must at all times seek to conceal the offense itself, regardless of the method through which this result is pursued.

Attempt

Paragraph e, which we have been discussing, after referring to concealment, adds "or in any other manner, in the commission or attempted commission."

The mention of commission of offenses appears to be redundant, since whenever reference is made to a classification of crimes, such an allusion refers to commission.

An attempted commission implies beginning to commit an offense, whenever the action is not completed for a reason unrelated to the desire of its principal. If the action is not completed due to the desire of the principal itself, it is not an attempted offense but rather an abandonment of the offense.

Attempts, in acts of corruption, may be quite frequent. They occur, for example, when someone offers a bribe to a public official and the official does not accept it or, on the contrary, when the official solicits a bribe and the private party refuses to pay it.

The draft of the paragraph is not ideal, however, insofar as it states: "attempted commission of . . . any of the acts referred to in this article," since article VI contains, in some cases, precisely, a description of an attempt. This is the case when we mention, in paragraph a, a "solicitation" and in paragraph b an "offer." In any case, the reference to offenses whose classifications were contained in the description of article VI is obvious.

Collaboration or Conspiracy

Both collaboration and conspiracy imply the agreement of two or more individuals to engage in acts of corruption. We must distinguish from these concepts the notions of coprincipal and participation or complicity, which require only that two or more individuals contribute to committing a single offense. By contrast, collaboration, as defined in many positive legal systems, instead defines an alignment of wills to undertake an indeterminate number of offenses. There may also be collaboration to conceal, such as, for example, when a corporation is created for legal purposes, but with the intent of using its structure to launder money.

"Conspiracy" implies the agreement of two or more individuals to commit a crime, but the terms may differ in various countries.

Inadequate Limitation

The end of paragraph e limits its scope to the actions described in article VI. Literally, this means that participation, concealment, attempts, etc., would only be considered as being acts of corruption if they refer to the conduct described in sections a, b, c, and d of that article.

But this limitation must not be interpreted literally, because one standard of a convention does not constitute a classification of crimes, and therefore, participation, concealment, and attempt must also be considered as being acts of corruption with respect to the offenses of transnational bribery and illegal enrichment as described in articles VIII and IX of the convention, indisputably as acts of corruption. The second paragraphs of articles VIII and IX support this interpretation, which is discussed in more detail in the section "'Offering,' 'Granting,' and Broader Forms of Adaptation," in the commentary to article VIII. Let us simply note that the concepts in paragraph e, when translated into positive law, are not even independent classifications of crimes but rather expanded forms of adaptation to the classification of crimes, and as such, correspond to the description of principal forms of conduct.

Application to Other Acts of Corruption

Section 2, article VI, provides that the ICAC "shall also be applicable by mutual agreement between or among two or more States Parties with respect to any other act of corruption not described herein."

This means that two or more states may assist each other in resolving situations arising from corrupt acts, committed or which have effects in either of those countries, although such acts might not coincide with any of those described in the articles of the convention.

The practical consequences of this stipulation are extremely important. Even if it does not involve the offense covered in the convention, one state may apply the ICAC's standards to give another state useful information for clarifying the offense, agreeing to a request to search for or seize evidence, processing and extradition (pursuant to article XIII), etc.

Despite the clarity of the section in question, two questions naturally arise:

1. Is it necessary for the agreement between two or more states with respect to the offenses to which the ICAC will apply to be expressed prior to the situation that led to that request for application or cooperation?
2. Is it necessary for the act of corruption that resulted in application of the convention to be legislated as an offense in the two states that propose to come to an agreement for such application?

The response is not simple and will depend upon the scope and flexibility with which the existing law in each state in question allows for cooperation.

Having made this qualification, we believe that simple assistance and cooperation, such as providing information, searching for evidence, etc., must not require prior agreement nor result in double incrimination; that is, it should not be necessary for the offense for which cooperation is requested to be legislated in both the requesting state and the requested state. For these purposes, it would seem sufficient that the classification of crimes exist in the requesting state, due to the previously mentioned principle of "ubi lex" (making no distinctions where the law does not make them).

The aforementioned section 2 mentions "mutual agreement," without requiring that it be prior to the acts that gave rise to it, and makes no reference to the principle of double incrimination.

Nevertheless, if the intended application of the ICAC involves extradition, the offense that gave rise to the request should be legislated in the two states, i.e., there must be double incrimination.

In this type of case, it is more difficult to answer the first question regarding the need for agreement prior to the event that originated the request, when the offense that gave rise to such request is not one included in articles VI, VIII, or IX of the ICAC; a case—of course—in which there would be double incrimination.

We believe that the response depends upon the case in question, with regard to the situations classified by article XIII of the ICAC. We will refer to the commentary of that article, because of the complexity of the issue.

ARTICLE VII

DOMESTIC LAW

The States Parties that have not yet done so shall adopt the necessary legislative or other measures to establish as criminal offenses under their domestic law the acts of corruption described in Article VI (1) and to facilitate cooperation among themselves pursuant to this Convention.

Obligation to Legislate

Article VII describes one of the main obligations assumed by the states parties in the ICAC. Clearly, this is the obligation to include within their respective legal systems the classification of crimes corresponding to the acts of corruption described in article VI. The word "establish," in the jargon of criminal law, aims to describe an illegal act and to assign it a penalty if the guilt of the individual who committed such act is proved.

The article discusses "legislative or other measures" to cover all possibilities deriving from the domestic mechanisms of each of the states. For example, in countries where, in addition to legislative penalties, it is also necessary for the executive branch to publish a decree, the state party will only comply with the ICAC when such decree is published and the provision is in full force as a law. If, in another case, a criminal law refers to the violation of an executive regulation, that regulation must be consistent with the commitments of the convention.

Obligation to Supplement Insufficient or Inadequate Legislation

The clause refers to "States Parties that have not yet done so" because in general, the concepts described in article VI correspond to offenses already provided for in domestic laws. However, such laws may be insufficient for the commitments of article VI, and if so, it would be necessary to supplement them. This would be the case, for example, if the criminal law of a country were to define bribery as related only to a case of delivering money and did not provide that the offering or acceptance of favors, promises, or advantages also be penalized, as the convention now requires.

In fact, there is one original commitment that arises from the combination of article VI and article I of the ICAC. Article I includes within the category of public official "those who have been selected, appointed, or elected to perform activities or functions in the name of the State or in the service of the State." This means that a bribe granted to an official who has been selected, appointed, or elected, even if he has not yet taken office, must be legally punished as such. The states parties have been forced to include this expansion of the definition of public official in their criminal laws. For the rest, we refer to the text contained in the commentary to article I.

Immediate Applicability?

Although article VII provides for the obligation to establish as offenses the acts of corruption described in article VI, within the domestic laws of each state, here we might briefly analyze the situation of those countries where, constitutionally, international treaties and agreements are immediately applicable. What happens in those cases? Are the acts of article VI automatically included as offenses within domestic law?

In general, we believe that in criminal matters, applicability is not immediate, because the principle of "no crime or punishment without prior law" is at stake. The convention's clauses do not strictly constitute a classification of crimes, because they contain generic descriptions and do not stipulate a penalty for each type of conduct in article VI. For it to be possible to apply a penalty, the most basic legal principles require not only that the illegal and culpable conduct be defined in a law prior to the event, but also that the penalty be established in that law.

On the other hand, the need for a positive law to expand the category of public official, pursuant to the terms of article I of the convention, is doubtful in the cases of existing classifications of crimes that include the notion of public official. We believe that in this case, it is necessary to examine some prior issues.

1. Of course, the issue refers only to states whose constitutions do not prevent the immediate applicability of international agreements, in which those agreements are comparable to a law or correspond to a superior hierarchy, since otherwise the need for a positive law that expands the category of "official" is indisputable.
2. In cases where the criminal law itself defines a public official in its classification, we believe that the existence of a law that changes that definition continues to be necessary, because of the principle of legality. Crime is a whole concept, and a classification includes not only a description of the act and the penalty, but also a description of the subject. Article VII establishes the commitment to adopt legislative measures to "establish as criminal offenses" acts of corruption under article VI. That is, there is an obligation to legislate when such acts of corruption do not exist as offenses, and such acts of corruption do not exist as offenses for individuals whom

the positive law itself does not consider as being public officials. However, we admit that the issue is open to debate, given the possible argument that the subsequent law changes prior law and the definition of public official that contains the classification of crimes is automatically expanded according to the terms of the convention. We believe, however, that legal security recommends the path of explicit legislation.

3. In cases where criminal law does not explicitly define public official and leaves the definition of this concept to doctrine, we believe that the convention is immediately operable. If doctrine is sufficient for introducing a definition included within the classification of crimes, then with all the more reason will a binding convention be suitable for such purpose. Therefore, in countries that have established, for example, a penalty for public officials who accept a bribe, but that have not defined public official, judges must extend coverage of the criminal law to the individuals included in article I of the convention.

4. Assuming the case of the preceding section, it remains to analyze what happens when a country's doctrine defines "public officials" only as the highest-level employees; for example, those with decision-making power or the authority to generate an administrative act by their signature. Most probably, the case will have no practical consequences. The offenses to which article VI refers are not those that may be committed solely by senior-level public servants, as is the case, for example, in some states that provide for the generic offense of "failure to fulfill one's duties as public official." Therefore, since the definition of article I of the ICAC applies solely "for the purposes of this Convention," the question is moot, at least for purposes of the scope of article VII, which we are analyzing here. Certainly, if there is an obligation to provide cooperation, extradition, or assistance, the broad definition of article I must be met.

Cooperation and Other Purposes

The original draft of article VII, as signed in Venezuela, did not contain the conjunction "and" between the phrase "establish as criminal offenses under their domestic law the acts of corruption described in Article VI (1)" and the phrase "to facilitate cooperation among themselves," which was added through a subsequent correction. Thus, the sense of the article was significantly different and more limited. The commitment to legislate classifications of crimes therefore appeared as related solely to the need to facilitate cooperation between the states.

Although cooperation between the states is one of the most important obligations of a convention, particularly the ICAC, what is no less important in the current context of the international order, is the need to promote legal security within each country of the hemisphere, because of all the arguments contained in the preamble, which have been explained in the chapters corresponding to their commentary. Peace, security, trade between nations, and human rights prevent us from closing our eyes to the domestic situations of the states, when those values are at risk. The absence of the "and" was undoubtedly an omission occurring sometime at the beginning of the document, but it was not in the clear spirit of its drafters, as expressed in the preamble and in the entire context of the ICAC.

To this end, after the signing of the convention and at the proposal of the United States, the "and" was added, as it now appears in the article, and it has thereby recovered its full meaning.

The Obligation Extends to Articles VIII and IX

As mentioned above, the obligation to legislate as established in article VII of the ICAC refers to the classification of crimes corresponding to the description of acts of corruption in article VI. This obligation to legislate has been defined fully and completely, with no conditions of any kind, because it was understood that no state could object to such basic and common concepts of criminal law as those contained in the aforementioned article VI.

However, the obligation to legislate classifications of crimes is not limited to the commitment of article VII. The texts of articles VIII and IX also contain the obligation to legislate as classifications of crimes the corrupt acts described in each of them.

Why, then, were those corrupt acts not included in article VI to thus be covered by the obligation to legislate in article VII?

Both the notion of "transnational bribery" as described in article VIII and that of "illegal enrichment" of article IX were extensively discussed during the Washington, D.C., meetings. Some representatives raised objections to the possibility of including those concepts within the positive legal systems of their respective countries, because of assumed problems of lack of constitutionality or lack of compatibility with the basic principles of their legal systems.

Given that situation, an original solution was adopted. The obligation was established of legislating such concepts; but that obligation is subject to compatibility of the transnational bribe or illegal enrichment with the constitution of the state proposing to legislate it, as well as with the basic principles of that state's legal system.

As may be seen, this is not a mere recommendation, but rather a binding commitment. The state must legislate as indicated above, but it is not required to do so if such an obligation conflicts with its basic legal principles.

Nevertheless, in a sense different from the one being analyzed, questions remain regarding the need to include a constitutional safeguard; that is, regarding the usefulness of introducing this condition, since the binding nature of the adaptation of any law or treaty to the constitution of a country would appear to be obvious, although the most modern international treaty criteria also call this statement into question.

Including the constitutionality clause within the specified context was necessary for political and legal reasons:

1. For international policy reasons, the conduct of a state that signs a commitment it cannot keep is not ideal nor does it demonstrate seriousness.
2. There are states that also have legal impediments to signing commitments that violate standards well-established in their legal traditions.

The condition introduced at the beginning of articles VIII and IX makes it possible for any state to approve the convention, insofar as it involves those articles, without violating its constitution and without incurring international liability, in the case of a failure to legislate that is justified by constitutional principles. This formula makes any reservation in this regard unnecessary.

ARTICLE VIII

TRANSNATIONAL BRIBERY[3]

Subject to its Constitution and the fundamental principles of its legal system, each State Party shall prohibit and punish the offering or granting, directly or indirectly, by its nationals, persons having their habitual residence in its territory, and businesses domiciled there, to a government official of another State, of any article of monetary value, or other benefit, such as a gift, favor, promise or advantage, in connection with any economic or commercial transaction in exchange for any act or omission in the performance of that official's public functions.

Among those States Parties that have established transnational bribery as an offense, such offense shall be considered an act of corruption for the purposes of this Convention.

Any State Party that has not established transnational bribery as an offense shall, insofar as its laws permit, provide assistance and cooperation with respect to this offense as provided in this Convention.

---

[3] For a wider study on this issue, see the book: Carlos Manfroni, *Soborno Transnacional* [Transnational Bribery], Abeledo-Perrot, Buenos Aires, 1998 (in Spanish).

An Offense against Free and Fair Competition

Article VIII is one of the most original of the ICAC.

A convention already plays an important role when it strengthens the effective application of existing positive law, through international legal solidarity. However, the ICAC introduces daring and innovative commitments, such as article VIII, which establishes the obligation to punish transnational bribery. The only legislative precedent to this concept, at the time the convention was assigned, was the United States' Foreign Corrupt Practices Act of 1977.

Until the ICAC, all laws naturally contained a penalty applying to bribes granted or offered to an official of that country; but none, outside the United States, had a regulation that would punish the bribing of a public official of another state.

To gain a precise idea of the nature of transnational bribery and the principles on which the penalties for such an offense must be based, is necessary to understand the historical reasons that make their existence possible and significant within the community of nations.

Within developing countries, countries in transition, and recently industrialized economies alone, capital flows increased from $15.2 billion in 1984 to over $173 billion in 1997.[4]

Between 1990 and 1996, direct foreign investment worldwide increased from $191 billion to almost $315 billion. But during this same period, in medium- and low-income countries, foreign direct investment increased from $24 billion to $120 billion.[5]

Total exports worldwide were $225 billion in 1968, rising to $5,546 billion in 1997.[6]

These figures and many others that might be provided show the explosive growth in trade and transnational investment in the last decade of the twentieth century. That growth, which is accelerating day by date due to the power of new communications, is of such a magnitude as to represent a qualitative and not merely quantitative leap in international relations.[7] A new political and economic era has arrived, in which the basic principles of capitalism and free enterprise have spread to almost the entire planet, but in addition, the practice of these principles has also been extended.

The big question in today's political world is not so much from what nations the capital originates, but in which country it settles, which is the same as asking where that capital will generate sources of employment and to which government will it pay taxes.

---

[4] International Monetary Fund, 1998 Annual Report.
[5] World Bank, World Development Indicators, 1998.
[6] International Monetary Fund, Intrnational Financial Statistics Yearbook.
[7] On this issue, please see: Carlos Manfroni: *Controll Político en el Capitalismo Global* [*Political Control in Global Capitalism*], (Buenos Aires: Abeledo-Perrot, 1999).

The new global capitalism, at least in theory, is capable of increasing people's living standards by disseminating new technology that makes possible — among many other things — improved medicine and higher food production. Similarly, international competition represents more opportunities for choice within each country, and therefore lower costs to governments and citizens, who are no longer prisoners of a few local suppliers. All too often, however, these effects are prevented by various actions that distort free competition, such as dumping and the corruption of governments and companies.

Full and effective operation of capitalism requires — by its very nature — the existence of free and fair competition. Respect for the rules of the market means that companies must compete only in terms of the price and quality of the goods and services they offer.

Bribery is one way of violating those principles of fair competition, whether it is used to induce a government to purchase the products of one company to the detriment of others, or when it is used to evade certain restrictions to which other companies are subject.

Transnational bribery is generally more serious than domestic bribery, for various reasons:

1. It is generally applied to contracts of very high amounts.
2. With respect to such contracts, people tend to have less true control power.
3. Upon spreading around the world, this offense seriously harms trust in the free market system and deters its real benefits.
4. The foreign residency of whoever is granting the bribe facilitates impunity.
5. It allows the enrichment of some national economies to the detriment of others; not only to the detriment of the economy of the country to which the bribed official belongs, but also to the detriment of the economies of the countries where companies reside that have been disqualified from competition because of a corrupt act.

It may be said, then, that there is a new value, the new legal system to be protected by the community of nations, which is free and fair competition in transnational trade.

It is true that the moral obligation to compete fairly has always existed, but only since the geographic growth of global trade has the affected reality acquired sufficient magnitude as to justify the attention of international law.

Thus, transparency, freedom, and fairness in international transactions together constitute the primary purpose sought to be protected by penalizing the bribing of foreign public officials.

It would be appropriate to at least take these considerations into account when analyzing the principles on which a state's jurisdiction and the prosecution of this offense are based.

Why a New Classification of Crimes?

Once we accept the need to legally protect free and fair competition in transnational transactions, we might still ask why it is necessary to create a criminal law that punishes someone who gives a bribe to a foreign public official. Is it not enough, for the specified purpose, to have laws in each country that punish the bribing of officials of that state itself?

Experience would appear to indicate that laws that suppress domestic bribery have not been sufficient, for various reasons.

In the first place, transnational bribery tends to be associated with transactions of large economic volume. This circumstance, in turn, is frequently linked to the corruption of a state's senior officials. Such officials often have a powerful influence on the administration and even the justice systems of their countries, and can make it difficult, if not impossible, for any investigation to succeed. Therefore, the governments to which bribed officials involved in a transnational operation belong may be less interested in criminalizing the bribe.

What is more, when the government whose officials were bribed shows a real interest in the investigation, the application of penalties to the active subject of the offense is difficult because of the domicile of the company or person who granted the bribe, outside the jurisdiction of the courts of the affected state. What is more, a request for extradition might be rejected with the argument as to the absence of the requirement of double incrimination, or, at least, that might be one possible interpretation.

But who could wish for a law that penalizes transnational bribery in the event of a lack of interest within the directly affected state or the government of the country where the company that granted the bribe is domiciled? The answer is: the countries of residence of companies competing in the global market that view themselves as harmed by the corrupt practices of those that do not respect the playing rules of the free market. Finally, the international community has an interest, since in this era of global trade, any economy may be affected by a lack of genuine competition. And that is precisely the reason why the commitment to legislate the bribery of foreign public officials has been assigned to the international level.

On December 17, 1997—one year after signing the Inter-American Convention against Corruption—the countries of the Organization for Economic Cooperation and Development (OECD) signed in Paris the Convention on Combating Bribery of Foreign Public Officials in International Commercial

Transactions.[8] This convention covers the world's largest exporters in America, Europe, and Asia. The example of the Organization of American States had fruitful results.

Precedents in Positive Law

Until the signing of the ICAC, the only precedent of article VIII in positive law was the United States' Foreign Corrupt Practices Act.[9] That regulation, signed in 1977 by the Carter administration and ratified by Congress, was a basic milestone in the history of world trade.

For the first time, a country established a penalty for private citizens, residents, and their businesses when they use bribery to penetrate foreign markets. It was a decision in which ethics prevailed over economic interests. The United States thereby took the risk of placing its businesses at a disadvantage compared to the businesses of other countries that were not penalized for foreign bribery. What is more, certain European states even allowed their businesses to write off bribes they paid to foreign governments on their tax returns, a policy that shows to what extent a government might consider bribery as being a practice that benefits its nation's economy. It is precisely this notion that serves as the basis for pressuring a government to assume a certain level of international responsibility for the conduct of its country's businesses, and consequently, to penalize transnational bribery rather than subsidize it.

The Foreign Corrupt Practices Act (FCPA) punishes bribery—or attempted bribery—when this illegal act is aimed at causing the action or influence of a public official of a foreign government, a political party, or a candidate for a political party of another country to obtain or retain business in the country to which the passive subject, i.e., the individual to whom the bribe is offered, belongs. It does not, however, punish bribery aimed at obtaining simple routine acts that are not used to obtain or retain business, which indicates—once again—that the law's purpose is merely to protect fair competition between businesses.

The FCPA's prohibition applies to private citizens—U.S. nationals or residents—and businesses—whether partnerships or corporations, joint ventures, legal entities, shareholder groups, or economic groups—provided that they maintain their principal place of business in the United States or are organized in accordance with the laws of that country.

The law and its penalties also extended to officials, directors, employees, or agents of the aforementioned businesses or shareholders when they are acting on behalf of those companies, as well as to issuers of securities registered on the U.S. stock market.

---

[8] The OECD Convention is analyzed in: Manfroni, *Soborno Transnacional* [Transnational Bribery], chapter 6.

[9] This law is analyzed in: Manfroni, *Soborno Transnacional* [Transnational Bribery], chapter 3.

Punishable activities include both promises and offers of bribes as well as authorizations to grant them. For the penalty to apply, it must be proved that a bribe granted by an employee of the business or a subsidiary of the corporation is linked—either actively or passively—to the parent company in the United States.

The penalties may be applied both to businesses themselves as well as to their officials and employees. For businesses, strong monetary penalties are provided for, which are applied by the federal courts, at the behest of the Department of Justice. There are also penalties to be applied by the Securities and Exchange Commission. Officials and employees may suffer both monetary penalties—which must be paid personally—as well as prison sentences.

In addition, various government agencies may disqualify businesses that have engaged in a specified illegal act from being suppliers.

It is precisely the possibility of penalizing businesses, and not merely their employees, that is the law's greatest dissuasive effect.

Constitution and Basic Principles

Article VIII of the ICAC contains, in essence, all elements of the U.S. Foreign Corrupt Practices Act. That article was created precisely as a consequence of a proposal from that country, which was supported by Argentina. However, several countries put up a certain resistance to one concept that, at the very least, extends beyond the principle of territoriality. That is why the article is headed by a safeguard clause.

As we have already noted in the final commentary to article VII, the obligation to legislate transnational bribery is subject to the absence of conflicts between the content of that commitment and the constitution and basic legal principles of each signatory country.[10]

In accordance with the good faith that must govern the interpretation of any pact (articles 26 and 31 of the Vienna Convention on the Law of Treaties), one must not abuse the interpretations on the extension of "basic principles." This category must cover all principles that, even if not included in national constitutions, are practically constitutional because of their nature. And even in this case we must once again take into consideration the good faith that must regulate the interpretation of treaties.

To this end, it does not appear sufficient to invoke territoriality as a basic principle that allows a country to avoid the commitment of article VIII. The principle of territoriality may come to be considered as a basic principle of a legal system of a country, like a type of "floor," but not as a "ceiling" to the possibility of exercising jurisdiction. This means that a country has the sovereign authority to try offenses committed on its territory and this authority is precisely what might

---

[10] See the section entitled: "The Obligation Extends to Articles VIII and IX," on page 53.

constitute a nondeclinable principle. But this argument cannot be used the other way around to prevent a broader than territorial jurisdiction from being exercised.

Moreover, the considerations discussed in the final section of the commentary to article VII shall apply to this issue.

Prohibit and Punish

The obligation assumed by states parties under article VIII is to prohibit and punish the acts of corruption described in that stipulation. There may be some doubt as to the usefulness of introducing the word "prohibit," when the wording also includes the word "punish." A penalty imposed by a regulation always implies prohibition. Nevertheless, the term "prohibit" appears to indicate that the transgression subject to the penalty applies to all fields of legal and economic relations and not just to the field of criminal law. What is more, the wording of the clause is an invitation to impose another type of restriction on companies that bribe foreign officials, in addition to the criminal penalty, such as those that have been adopted in the U.S. precedent.

"Offering," "Granting," and Broader Forms of Adaptation

The act that must be prohibited and penalized, according to the commitment of article VIII, is that of directly or indirectly offering or granting a bribe. This description includes both the action (granting) and the attempt (offering) as well as participation, which is implied in the term "indirectly."

It may be arguable whether the commitment, in departing from article VI, varied from paragraph e of that article, which included among corrupt acts complicity, concealment, instigation, etc. In view of this situation, we should note that the link between article VIII and article VI is implicit and that no state may claim otherwise to avoid punishing those forms of participating in the offense of transnational bribery. This is so because the concepts included in paragraph e of article VI are not independent classifications of crimes but rather dependent forms of the principal offense. Thus, when a state has agreed to legislate a classification of crimes, it has also agreed to include in its laws accessory notions such as complicity, concealment, instigation, etc.

In any case, the reasoning of the preceding paragraph is almost unnecessary, for two reasons:

1. When a state legislates a classification of crimes, that classification of crimes is included within its general legislation, which in all countries includes participation, attempt, concealment, instigation, etc., as forms applying to all offenses.

2. The second paragraph of article VIII itself provides that "among those States Parties that have established transnational bribery as an offense, such offense shall be considered an act of corruption for the purposes of this Convention." Defining transnational bribery as an act of corruption automatically implies its comparison to the acts described in article VI, including—of course—the application of paragraph e of that article.

Nationals, Residents, and Domiciled Businesses

The law that each country must decree in fulfillment of article VIII of the ICAC must apply to nationals, residents, and domiciled businesses in the legislating country, which will be the one that exercises jurisdiction when one of the specified subjects bribes an official of a foreign state.

At the time it gives legal status to those commitments or, as the case may be, those of the OECD convention, it may be important to consider what jurisdiction criteria will be applied by a country that intends to punish transnational bribery. This analysis would be particularly useful for evaluating the extension to be applied—at all times for purposes of punishment—to the category of "nationals, residents, and domiciled businesses" in a country.

In criminal law there are various criteria for determining to whom a state can or must, and in what cases, extend its punitive power.

The principle of territoriality is the most common one, and consists in applying criminal law to offenses committed within the very territory of the legislating country. All countries recognize this principle, at a minimum, as being the most important basis for applying their laws.

The principle of "legal status" or "active nationality" is less developed throughout the world. This is the basis used by countries that punish their domestic citizens for offenses committed anywhere, even if not on their own territory.

The "real" or "defense" principle supports the extension of criminal law to offenses committed outside the national territory but that have effects on that territory. The typical academic example is that of counterfeiting; an act that, although performed outside the country, affects the national economy.

Finally, certain offenses that affect the "law of nations" or whose enforcement is in the interest of every nation equally tend to fall within the principle of the "universality" of criminal law. In some cases, the nation that has captured a criminal may be acknowledged as having the authority to try his offenses, or else, in the case of specific acts such as war crimes or genocide, action under international jurisdiction is called for.

What principle will apply to transnational bribery law?

An initial reading of article VIII of the ICAC and its precedent, the FCPA, appears to indicate a clear adoption of the principle of active nationality.

Nevertheless, a few examples—among many possible ones—would demonstrate that the solution is not so easy.

If a foreign citizen is a director at the parent company of a company domiciled in the country and authorizes a bribe in a foreign country, it would seem clear that the law should include him in its punishment, even if he is not a national. What should apply, on the other hand, in the case of a national who is an employee of a foreign company domiciled abroad who grants a bribe to an official of a third country on behalf of that company? In this case, the jurisdiction of the country of which the employee is a citizen does not appear to be so reasonable. On the contrary, a law that would penalize a foreign manager of a company domiciled in the country does appear to be logical and consistent with the convention's commitment, when that manager grants a bribe to a public official of another state. And these examples still do not take into consideration companies comprising joint public/private ownership or domestic interests in foreign companies.

What is more, the Foreign Corrupt Practices Act itself does not crudely apply the principle of nationality, but rather requires, for its application, the existence of a link between the employee that granted the bribe and the parent company in the United States. In this case, we have touched upon a principle of extended territoriality, which appears to be erroneous, because territoriality cannot be extended to another country.

Nor does the real or defense principle appear to apply, as it is designed rather to judge direct attacks experienced by a state as a political organization, such as counterfeiting or conspiracy against its authorities.

In addition, any attempt to apply the principle of universality would conflict with the necessary jurisdiction of the state over the nationality, domicile, or residence of the individuals or legal entities that committed the offense, in accordance with the ICAC.

In our opinion, legislation generated based on the ICAC or the OECD convention should not ignore the historical reasons or the moral and philosophical causes for which such commitments were stipulated. It is very difficult to force the application of old principles of jurisdiction, conceived in a stage of states closed in upon themselves, at a time when nations can no longer conceive of themselves as being disconnected from the international political community and the world business community.

If it is agreed that punishing transnational bribery is aimed at protecting free and fair international trade competition, the reason the state must punish its nationals or its companies is based on the acknowledgment of a certain level of political responsibility for them.

In classic jurisdiction principles, the state projects its power toward orbits it recognizes as being its own—its territory, its nationals, its defense—solely to preserve the interests of its community. On the other hand, one might distinguish situations that the state accepts in their universality, but with respect to which it excludes itself or has been excluded from their jurisdiction.

Transnational bribery is a new principle, which we might refer to as "international responsibility" or by any other appropriate name, to describe the role the state is currently called upon to play as part of the community of nations. The state acknowledges situations in which an international legal good is affected, but in the creation of which it has some objective responsibility, because the events were instigated by its nationals under certain conditions, or encouraged from its territory, or were carried out through structures organized in accordance with its laws or by individuals who assisted it through their taxes.

The state, therefore, by exercising its jurisdiction, becomes politically and objectively coresponsible for protecting a common international good. If this basis is accepted, it will perhaps be easier to establish the limits of its jurisdiction.

Benefit Offered or Granted

With respect to benefits offered or granted to a public official of another country in the form of a bribe, the text of the article repeats the wording with which article VI describes traditional bribery in its active form.

Naturally, the commitment to punish transnational bribery cannot include the passive subject, who is the public official of a foreign country who has been bribed.

With respect to the type and extent of the benefit, we will therefore refer to our commentary on article VI, section 1(b).

Economic or Commercial Transactions

The existence of transnational bribery, as it pertains to the convention, requires that all conditions described in this commentary occur within the context of an economic or commercial transaction. This means that not just any bribe granted to a public official of a foreign state will constitute transnational bribery. In fact, the Foreign Corrupt Practices Act excludes bribes granted to perform merely routine acts.

These limitations are logical and once again are indicative of the nature of transnational bribery, which focuses, as an offense, against free and fair competition and not as an offense against a foreign government.[11]

---

[11] See the beginning of the commentary to article VIII: "An Offense Against Free and Fair Competition," on page 55.

The punishment of any offense, as has already been noted, is oriented toward protecting a legal good. The punishment of traditional bribery seeks to protect the integrity of the government of the state itself. But punishing transnational bribery does not seek to protect the government of a foreign state, since it does not follow that one state should provide criminal protection for the government of another. The legal good that is protected by prohibiting the bribing of foreign public officials is the proper order of international business, free and fair competition in transnational trade.

The intent of punishing transnational bribery is merely to create a level and identical world trade playing field for all competitors to be subject to the same conditions. Article 15, section 1, of the OECD convention, which is specifically intended for punishing the bribery of foreign public officials, represents the best proof of the specified purpose. That clause states that the convention "shall enter into force on the sixtieth day following the date upon which five of the ten countries which have the ten largest export shares, and which represent by themselves at least sixty per cent of the combined total exports of those ten countries, have deposited their instruments of acceptance, approval, or ratification."

It is quite clear, from reading that clause, that the intent is to establish identical rules between exporting countries that have not wished to commit to punishing transnational bribery until their principal competitors did the same, with the exception of the United States, which had already had those penalties since 1977.

If transnational bribery were not limited to economic or commercial transactions, a state would have to extend its jurisdiction to punish any of its nationals who offered a bribe to a police agent of another country just to avoid a fine for a traffic violation.

Certainly, any bribe of a foreign public official will always be a bribe for the state to which the suborned official belongs, even if it does not involve an economic or commercial transaction. But bribery is one thing, and transnational bribery is something very different, even though sometimes both classifications of crimes focus on the same action.

With regard to the scope that must be assigned to the expression "economic or commercial transaction," a few clarifications are in order. A transaction involves a business, contract, agreement, exchange, etc. According to current use, the very word "transaction" implies a monetary sense; nevertheless, the wording explicitly states that the transaction must be economic or commercial in nature. This eliminates, therefore, agreements that are merely cultural, political, or military, unless such agreements have commercial clauses.

During the meeting of the style committee, which was held the night prior to the signing of the convention, there was discussion as to whether the article should read "economic or commercial transaction" or simply "commercial transaction" or "economic transaction." The expressions would appear to be somewhat redundant.

A phrase was also proposed that stated "commercial or financial transaction," in order for the expression to not be redundant and to explicitly include banking activities.

Nevertheless, the words "economic" and "commercial" were retained for two reasons that should be examined together:

1. Economic transactions involve financial transactions.
2. The style committee did not consider itself as having the authority to change the proposal, as it was drafted, and of course there was no time for a new consultation, with only a few hours until the signing.

It remains to be determined whether the classification of the offense of transnational bribery requires that the foreign state necessarily be one of the parties to the economic or commercial transaction. In other words, does transnational bribery exist only when a foreign government is induced to purchase specific goods or services? What would happen in the case of a transaction carried out only between private companies, but whose success depended upon permission being granted by a foreign state? What about the case of a large business corporation that calls for international bids from supplier companies that have specific government quality certifications from among which that corporation will make its purchase? If one of the potential suppliers were to gain such a certificate through a bribe, could this be considered transnational bribery?

The solution to this question will depend, of course, on the limits established by each law, and fulfillment of their commitments under the agreement. But this does not yet answer the question as to which law best satisfies the commitments in this regard. Neither the precedent of the FCPA nor the subsequent definition contained in the OECD convention afford a final response.

The FCPA punishes the bribery of foreign public officials for purposes of inducing an official to help obtain or retain business or to direct business toward another party. The OECD convention has quite a similar wording and includes bribes granted to obtain improper advantages within the context of international business.

Although the historical intent of international commitments in even the laws of the United States appears to have been focused solely on transactions involving governments as a commercial party, nothing prevents these provisions from applying to business deals between private companies when an action by a government official is necessary to obtain or retain business. This interpretation would be based on the Latin principle usually referred to as "ubi lex," which states that no distinctions should be made where the law does not do so.

Full Functioning of the Agreement

Paragraph two of article VIII, as we already noted, provides that "among those States Parties that have established transnational bribery as an offense, such offense shall be considered an act of corruption for the purposes of this Convention."

This clause, which is symmetrical with another that refers to illicit enrichment, implies that all effects corresponding to the acts of article VI and all consequences of the convention that apply to transnational bribery, such as the articles on extradition, assistance and cooperation, precautionary measures, etc., apply to transnational bribery

In the event of the inability of any state to legislate this classification of crimes because of the constitutional safeguard appearing at the beginning of article VIII, or inaction by other states under an inadequate claim of such safeguard, or simple negligence, the ICAC was not intended to prevent the beneficial effects of the article among countries that have introduced it into their laws.

In fact, this clause is to the benefit solely of the possibility of extradition, because the other consequences, such as assistance and cooperation, as it were, precautionary measures, and the prohibition on claiming bank secrecy, are included in the assistance and cooperation obligation, which the following paragraph establishes more widely for all states parties.

Assistance and Cooperation

The final paragraph of article VIII, which is similar to another one corresponding to illicit enrichment, contains a regulation that is very useful for the purposes of the ICAC, insofar as it stipulates that "any State Party that has not established transnational bribery as an offense shall, insofar as its laws permit, provide assistance and cooperation with respect to this offense as provided in this Convention."

If we take into consideration the fact that international assistance and cooperation are of fundamental importance in investigating and punishing this type of offense, and if we also consider the scope of these tasks as contained in the convention, we will realize the importance of the aforementioned paragraph. As we have already noted, in the ICAC assistance and cooperation cover not only the obligations of article XIV, but also those of articles XV and XVI.

The scope of this paragraph goes so far as to state that if the state party to which the official bribed by a foreign company belongs has not legislated transnational bribery within its domestic law, it must provide the assistance and cooperation required by the domicile state of the company that granted the bribe, if the latter state has adopted this legislation.

The phrase "insofar as its laws permit," which is introduced at the end of the article, like the one corresponding to illicit enrichment, fulfills a condition that some states requested to support those paragraphs. However, it must be interpreted that the refusal to give assistance and cooperation cannot be based on an arbitrary law nor decreed subsequently to the convention for purposes of avoiding this commitment.

Of course, the absence of such laws must be considered as being favorable to fulfillment of the agreement.

Final Considerations on the Article's Purposes

This clause, therefore, clearly expresses the will of the states parties to preserve transparency and fairness in international trade, with a view to an increasingly competitive world economy, in the expansion of which tolerance for corrupt practices would raise frictions between companies and countries and increase people's costs, to levels intolerable for coexistence.

Transnational corruption is an ingredient external to capitalism and causes many evils that are erroneously attributed to the system, because they are not based on an excess of competition, but rather on its negation or alteration, to the benefit of corrupt companies and to the detriment of parties with fewer resources, who suffer from the additional costs resulting from the bribes and the poor decisions of their governments.

Nevertheless, the spread of corrupt practices such as transnational bribery, monopolistic or oligopolistic activities, and dumping discredit not only the free market but also, in general, any system based on the recognition of personal freedoms.

America's example, in applying penalties to the corrupt alteration of trade, is the first precedent of an international agreement to set fairer playing rules for trade. The subsequent signing of the OECD convention, and above all, the fulfillment of both commitments by the states, will help to build the basic weapons for a legal fight aimed at freeing people from the unfair costs they so often bear for the goods and services acquired by their governments.

ARTICLE IX

ILLICIT ENRICHMENT

Subject to its Constitution and the fundamental principles of its legal system, each State Party that has not yet done so shall take the necessary measures to establish under its laws as an offense a significant increase in the property of a government official that he cannot reasonably explain in relation to his lawful earnings during the performance of his functions.

Among those States Parties that have established illicit enrichment as an offense, such offense shall be considered an act of corruption for the purposes of this Convention.

Any State Party that has not established illicit enrichment as an offense shall, insofar as its laws permit, provide assistance and cooperation with respect to this offense as provided in this Convention.

An Offense against Transparency

The current wording of article IX corresponds to a proposal from Argentina, the Criminal Code of which has included this item for over three decades. The proposal was initially supported by certain Latin American countries, such as Peru, Venezuela, Mexico, and Colombia, among others, but it generated certain resistance among the Anglo Saxon countries, whose representatives believed they might have a problem with the article's constitutionality (see "An Unconstitutional Offense?" beginning on page 70).

Precisely to prevent this, other proposals were suggested. The United States and Jamaica submitted a draft making the corrupt act in question comparable to benefiting from or concealing property originating from crimes of corruption. But this clearly involved completely different aspects that were already included in the clause on concealment or laundering.

With a view to reconciling the positions, Mexico presented two alternate drafts. One focused on falsification of the property declaration, for purposes of concealing illicit enrichment. The second suggestion was similar to misappropriation of public funds.

The closest proposal to the one that was finally adopted was that of Colombia, which defined illicit enrichment as "an unjustified increase in property obtained by an individual who performs a public function, by reason of his position or duties, and to the detriment of the State patrimony." In our view, however, this proposal remained subject to the problem of requiring proof of harm of the state's patrimony, a circumstance that is not required even by the ICAC for any case, as clearly stated in its article XII. By contrast, an official may illicitly enrich himself from his position, without detriment to the state patrimony; for example, when he demands bribes to perform his duties or tasks he is required to perform in accordance with his functions. Or he may enrich himself through means completely unrelated to the illegitimate performance of his duties, but which do involve other offenses unrelated to the government.

After holding many conversations and meetings outside the general discussion, an agreement was arrived at by which the Anglo Saxon countries accepted the Argentine draft, subject to insertion of the constitutional safeguard that appears at the beginning.

We believe that this wording is the one that satisfies the intended purposes, to preserve transparency of the public function.

During the general discussions, we noted that the concept of illicit enrichment is particularly useful for the people of Latin America, whose states frequently lack the effective high-technology resources to detect offenses at the precise moment they occur. We also noted that this weakness is combined with mockery of the law in the form of the material ostentation demonstrated by their officials, with the people having no means of determining on what particular occasion, out of the thousands available to public agents, an offense was committed, or even the innumerable offenses that gave rise to the enrichment.

There are many ways of combating corruption. Some aim at its sources, and involve administrative systems and prevention. These are undoubtedly the best, but we see no reason why any remedy must be rejected. Others are aimed at individuals and involve criminal sanctions. This is not the best solution, but it is a necessary path, without which prevention itself is lacking in basis.

The concept of illicit enrichment belongs to the second category of methods, but may be easily linked to a preventive measure, the property declaration by officials (article III, section 4).

This is the classification of crimes that most completely corresponds to the effects of the offense, as it is aimed directly at the purpose that the corrupt official pursued, the acquisition and display of property.

It might be assumed, perhaps, that the notion of a corrupt official who displays his property without fear of exposure and consequences is of the utmost ingenuousness. Someone will undoubtedly note that proceeds from corruption are generally channeled into secret accounts.

The reality is that this method is not ingenuous. It is possible for a corrupt official to derive a good part of the ill-gotten money from secret accounts, but it is highly unlikely that he will content himself with spending so little of that money as to not be noticed.

No one robs for his grandchildren. The personality of a temperate, austere man who lives moderately while saving for future generations is not exactly that of a corrupt official. If a corrupt official had such discipline and virtues, he would very probably not be corrupt. Certainly any estimate, particularly when sociology is involved, has its exceptions. But the law is based on general cases, rather than on exceptions.

The crime of illicit enrichment, combined with a good system of asset declarations that includes the obligation to register promises of sale or donation made in favor of public officials by their consumers or straw men, under penalty of annulment, is an extremely useful weapon against corruption and money laundering.

An Unconstitutional Offense?

It was precisely the preventive actions generated with respect to the crime of illicit enrichment that were the motive behind including in article IX the condition "subject to its Constitution and the fundamental principles of its legal system." Later, this same paragraph was applied to transnational bribery. This means that the state is not required to legislate illicit enrichment if it justifiably demonstrates that this classification of crimes is a violation of its constitutional system, without need to make any exceptions to the ICAC.

However, is illicit enrichment an unconstitutional offense? There are numerous and very well prepared works that claim this position, with well-founded reasoning. In essence, all of them are based on two arguments:

1. The opposition to the principle of innocence, with the consequent reversal of the burden of proof, in requiring the accused party to demonstrate the legal source of his property
2. Violation of the guarantee against self-incrimination, also because of the need to explain the source of one's property

Despite the merit and the clarity of those arguments, we believe that their error consists in viewing illicit enrichment solely as an indication of other offenses against the government, traditionally deeply rooted in law, such as bribery, fraud, etc.

It is quite certain that most probably a party accused of illicit enrichment has arrived at the position of which he is accused through certain other offenses against the government. Or perhaps not.

Some legal experts who oppose legislation relating to illicit enrichment maintain, for example, that the accused party could have been enriched through another type of illegal activity, such as drug trafficking, clandestine betting, etc., and nevertheless, he would be subject to a penalty corresponding to an offense against the government. They also raise the extreme case of the confession of such offenses to justify the source of the property, with a view to demonstrating the absurd situation to which the court would be subject, in requiring it to elect the classification of crimes to apply.

We believe that the constitutionality of illicit enrichment will not be understood until this notion is included as an independent criminal classification.

A state has every right to require that government officials only own property they can justify through their legal activities, for reasons of administrative transparency, public trust, and criminal policy. Therefore, if the state stipulates a penalty for those officials whose property does not correspond to their lawful earnings, it violates no constitutional principle. This legislative policy is no threat against equality, because such a constitutional guarantee only imposes consistent treatment on similar situations.

But public officials are in special positions, which are more demanding than those applying to other citizens.

For this reason, when an official shows property significantly greater than would be expected, given his lawful earnings, the establishment of another classification of crimes should not be expected. The offense consists precisely in possessing gains not justified as lawful.

It does not appear to be excessive for a community to ask that its government officials have only the property they can lawfully justify. And in any event, if this does seem to be an exaggerated policy, this alleged exaggeration falls within the framework of a criminal policy that, like all policies, is subject to different opinions. But this is not unconstitutional.

Within this framework, it matters little whether the unjustified property originated from an act against the government or from drug trafficking, clandestine gambling, or the thousand possible variables one might imagine. The community punishes a lack of transparency by its administrators.

Demonstrable Lawful Earnings

As we have noted, the community is entitled to demand transparency in its officials' earnings. It is reasonable to seek to have public agents who can demonstrate the basis of their standards of living. In that context, such a demonstration also forms part of the conditions for legitimacy. No one is in a better position than the official to demonstrate that. There is no reason why, in a state governed by the rule of law, a person cannot justify his earnings.

We repeat that this is not a reversal of the burden of truth that requires a public servant to demonstrate that he did not commit an offense. Simply stated, a failure to demonstrate this constitutes a classification of crimes. Demonstration is not subsequent to the offense. If it can be demonstrated, the employee cannot even be accused.

There are countries in which the possession of weapons without a permit from specific authorities is an offense. It would not occur to anyone that the need to show such a permit would be a reversal of the burden of proof. The same thing applies to tax regulations in many states.

When mention is made of "lawful earnings during the performance of his functions" it is clear that this covers all earnings the official receives for his functions or outside of them, provided that the outside earnings are not incompatible with his position. For that reason, the article states: "during the performance of his functions" rather than "based on the performance of his functions."

Regarding the time during which this measurement must take place, the ICAC requires, at least, that the period begin when the official has been "selected, appointed or elected," even if he has not yet assumed his duties (see commentary to article I).

Although his functions end when an official leaves his position for any reason, this does not mean that the discovery of apparently subsequent enrichment that demonstrably occurred during the performance of his duties does not fall within the category of illicit enrichment. But the consideration of these terms and the methods of determining them corresponds to each country's administrative and criminal policy.

Increase in Wealth

To measure increased wealth, we must take into consideration not only increases in assets but also reductions in liabilities. If an official cannot justify the payment of a large debt with his lawful earnings, this circumstance is equivalent to acquiring property.

The decision regarding the scope of control of the official's direct family members is left up to each country's administrative and criminal policy. In general, control systems take into consideration at least increases in the property of the spouse and minor children who are dependents of the agent.

We believe that a good monitoring system should include promises of sale, donation, or sale orders made in favor of public officials by individuals contributing to the concealment of property, which is a method that corrupt employees use to ensure the return of property in the possession of their accomplices after the fact.

Significant Excess

Not just any increase in wealth in excess of an official's lawful earnings must be taken into consideration for illicit enrichment. It must be a significant excess, large and demonstrable; we would almost say: gross.

If officials are required to demonstrate their earnings with complete accuracy, this would be an excessively burdensome load, an obsessive preoccupation that would conspire against the peace of mind and balance they require to perform their functions effectively. At the same time, a requirement of such a nature would become a political weapon through which adversaries would mutually accuse one other, in the hopes of finding in each other some minimum difference in property that, perhaps because of carelessness or negligence, they were unable to justify.

Full Functioning of the Agreement

As with the offense of transnational bribery, the ICAC applies with all its effects among the states that have defined illicit enrichment. In reality, the second paragraph of article IX, like the third paragraph, was created for illicit enrichment and both were afterward applied as well to transnational bribery.

There are several countries in Latin America whose legal structures already included the notion of illicit enrichment, such that among them the ICAC may fully apply, including the standards on extradition.

Furthermore, we refer to the comments we made in the corresponding section in the commentary to article VIII.

Assistance and Cooperation

Illicit enrichment is one of the criminal concepts with respect to which assistance and cooperation are most important. Very frequently, officials who illicitly enrich themselves seek to conceal their property by acquiring property in countries other than their own, or deposits in foreign bank accounts.

In general, the governments of countries that receive this type of property are not particularly enthusiastic about identifying their sources, since these are investments that pay taxes and contribute to development.

However, the ICAC includes an obligation to cooperate, which, although appearing in numerous treaties, on the one hand has broader features (see the commentary to article XIV) and on the other hand, due to the number of countries that have committed to be bound by and support the Organization of American States, has acquired extraordinary political force.

With respect to this section as well, we refer to its corresponding section in the commentary to article VIII.

ARTICLE X

NOTIFICATION

When a State Party adopts the legislation referred to in paragraph 1 of articles VIII and IX, it shall notify the Secretary General of the Organization of American States, who shall in turn notify the other States Parties. For the purposes of this Convention, the offenses of transnational bribery and illicit enrichment shall be considered acts of corruption for that State Party thirty days following the date of such notification.

Article X arose because of a proposal from the Argentine Foreign Ministry, relating to the basic need to know among which states this ICAC will begin to apply fully with respect to the offenses of transnational bribery and illicit enrichment.

By contrast, due to the obligation of the states parties to adopt laws corresponding to the acts of corruption provided for in article VI, without conditions or safeguards, it was not considered necessary to provide notification on such fulfillment. If a state that had not legislated any of the crime classifications provided for in article VI had not fulfilled the commitment of article VII (Obligation to Legislate), it could be subject to an international legal action.

As may be seen, a state party that has legislated on transnational bribery and illicit enrichment must provide notification of such fact to the Secretary General of the Organization of American States who, in turn, notifies the other states parties. Thirty days after this final notification, those offenses are considered as being acts of corruption for the ICAC's purposes. This means that the convention applies fully in their regard, including its relationship to the wider forms of adaptation of the classification of crimes as set forth in section 1(e) of the ICAC and extradition.

ARTICLE XI

PROGRESSIVE DEVELOPMENT

1. *In order to foster the development and harmonization of their domestic legislation and the attainment of the purposes of this Convention, the States Parties view as desirable, and undertake to consider, establishing as offenses under their laws the following acts:*

   a) *The improper use by a government official or a person who performs public functions, for his own benefit or that of a third party, of any kind of classified or confidential information which that official or person who performs public functions has obtained because of, or in the performance of, his functions.*

   b) *The improper use by a government official or a person who performs public functions, for his own benefit or that of a third party, of any kind of property belonging to the State or to any firm or institution in which the State has a proprietary interest, to which that official or person who performs public functions has access because of, or in the performance of, his functions.*

   c) *Any act or omission by any person who, personally or through a third party, or acting as an intermediary, seeks to obtain a decision from a public authority whereby he illicitly obtains for himself or for another person any benefit or gain, whether or not such act or omission harms State property.*

   d) *The diversion by a government official, for purposes unrelated to those for which they were intended, for his own benefit or that of a third*

> *party, of any movable or immovable property, monies or securities be-*
> *longing to the State, to an independent agency, or to an individual, that*
> *such official has received by virtue of his position for purposes of ad-*
> *ministration, custody or for other reasons.*
>
> 2. *Among those States Parties that have established these offenses, such offenses*
>   *shall be considered acts of corruption for the purposes of this Convention.*
> 3. *Any State Party that has not established these offenses shall, insofar as its*
>   *laws permit, provide assistance and cooperation with respect to these of-*
>   *fenses as provided in this Convention.*

Binding Force

Article XI consists of a very special category of commitment within the ICAC. As may be seen, it is a description of a number of acts of corruption that the states parties acquired a certain obligation to introduce within their criminal legislation as types of action to which a penalty corresponds. However, it is clear that those acts did not fall within the same category as described in article VI, and therefore, they are not covered by the obligation to legislate to the degree provided for in article VII. In article VII, the states committed to legislating the acts of corruption provided for in article VI, with no conditions. This is the maximum degree of commitment assumed with respect to the obligation to create legislation.

Nor is it an obligation subject to the condition that the legislation to be created be compatible with the constitution of each state and the basic principles of each legal system, as in the case of transnational bribery and illicit enrichment.

Article XI is a third category of commitment, of a level lower than the obligations arising from articles VI and VII, and even lower than the commitment of articles VIII and IX, but more advanced than the one engaged in article III, by which states are only required to consider measures (although this obligation must also be interpreted in good faith and not as an opportunity to indefinitely avoid application of the principles it contains).

The need to create this intermediate level of obligation arose as a result of a contingent situation. The description of the concepts contained in paragraphs a, b, c, and d was drafted from the Washington meetings; but that draft had arrived at the Caracas meeting without the application of a specific degree of commitment on the part of the states parties.

During the meeting of a working group formed at the last minute, the Chilean delegation insisted, quite rightly, and was supported by the Argentine delegation, on the need to compare the concepts of article XI to the acts of corruption contained in article VI; that is, to commit the states to the maximum degree of obligation to legislate those acts as classifications of crimes. However, a disagreement arose with other delegations, which seemed to be unable to be resolved, despite the late hour and the proximity of the time for signing the document. Nor was there support for the idea of making the acts contained in article XI comparable to the type of obligation imposed for transnational bribery and illicit enrichment.

Nevertheless, the acts described in the article known as "Progressive Development" appeared to be too important as to make them solely dependent upon an absolutely free decision by the states parties.

We therefore suggested a wording that all parties to this dispute accepted with greater or lesser enthusiasm: "the States Parties view as desirable, and undertake to consider."

It was not, as one may see, an unconditional obligation. Nor was it an obligation subject solely to the measures' constitutionality. But the commitment is higher than a mere promise to "consider."

The mere obligation to consider the adoption of measures includes the possibility of judging the value of those measures. Under such an assumption, a state party might not adopt them because it does not believe they are desirable for the purposes of the convention or its legal system, although we believe that this freedom must also be subject to an evaluation of reasonableness and there may not be absolutely unfounded opposition (articles 26 and 31 of the Vienna Convention on the Law of Treaties).

Within the context of the commitment of article XI, on the other hand, the states parties already made their value judgment and deemed it desirable to adopt the concept it described. Provided that they have adopted that formula, they are prohibited from claiming that the legislation contained in the article is not desirable for their systems or for the ICAC's purposes. And they have said that they "view as desirable, and undertake to consider, establishing as offenses under their laws." And if the grounds of lack of suitability cannot be claimed, there are not many arguments left to resist adopting the stipulated legislation. Perhaps this is an opportunity. No other one occurs to us.

But the argument of opportunity cannot last forever. At some point, the states that have not adopted this legislation must do so.

Use of Classified Information

The description of the concept of paragraph a is very clear. All states hold certain types of information that is legally classified, for reasons of security, intelligence, high technology, or to the benefit of an investigation, etc. There are also some types of information to which only specific officials have access, because of the nature of their tasks. This may be, for example, economic data of extreme value to business owners or securities traders, who may take advantage of their competitors through their knowledge of such data.

Paragraph a requires that the individual who improperly uses the information be a public official. It is not necessary that the official who uses the classified information have access to it because his functions are closely related to those of the comptroller or to handling that information. It could involve an official in another area of the government who has received comments from another agent or who has been directly informed of the matter due to some one-time circumstance. For this reason, the text reads: "classified or confidential information [he] has obtained because of, or in the performance of, his functions."

For the act to be included in paragraph a, there must be a benefit deriving from using the information. The wording of that stipulation explicitly states that it may be to the benefit of an official or a third party. That third party could be a private individual or another public official. Information obtained through an employee of an agency that monitors the stock market, supplied to a securities agent, constitutes typical bad faith to the benefit of a private individual. On the other hand, if an official is being investigated by a government intelligence agency and another employee warns him of that fact, such behavior would also represent an improper use of classified information, but in favor of a public official.

The benefit may be economic or noneconomic. A noneconomic benefit may be obtained, for example, when certain expected information on the topics of a state university examination are improperly provided to a student by some professor or employee of that university or other agency.

Nor is it necessary, according to the text, that the official receive a bribe in exchange for the information provided. This circumstance would place the public employee in the situation of article VI.

Of course, according to article XII, the behavior described in article XI does not require that the state suffer harm to its property.

One of the duties of the government is fairness, and it is therefore for good reason that the use of reserved or privileged information to the benefit of the official himself, of other officials or private individuals, constitute an act of corruption.

Use of State Property

The use of state property for purposes other than it was intended falls under section 1(b) of the article on progressive development. We believe that this concept must be included among the acts of corruption of article VI, since it involves an offense that in many countries exists under the name "misappropriation of public funds."

As in the preceding case, it is not necessary that the party benefited be the official himself, nor, according to article XII, is it required that state property be harmed. The use of a city's equipment to grade private land, for example, falls within this description, even if the land belongs to a third party and the equipment that was used suffered not the least harm.

Certainly, one must assume a certain degree of flexibility in the case law of the various states in interpreting standards similar to the one described above. Otherwise, a simple telephone call from a place of public employment to the employee's home could constitute an act of corruption. Although, perhaps, a call to another country that is unrelated to the job and involves a certain expense to the state could indeed be considered a corrupt act. As in all cases, the law must be clarified by common sense, which helps to distinguish one circumstance from another, as well as a certain range of intermediate actions that may be classified as "ethical shortfalls" but not offenses.

Illicit Acquisition of a Benefit

Paragraph c, Section 1, article XI, contains a description of a sui generis classification of acts that do not correspond precisely to traditional offenses against the government. It involves behavior by a private individual who seeks "to obtain a decision from a public authority whereby he illicitly obtains for himself or for another person any benefit or gain, whether or not such act or omission harms State property."

This paragraph arose as a consequence of a proposal from the Venezuelan delegation, which, with good reason, was particularly sensitive to the harm that had been caused to the state by a group of bankers from that country. It must not be forgotten that the ICAC itself arose as a result of a project by Venezuelan President Rafael Caldera.

That description seeks to cover conduct that, although not involving a bribe, is aimed at obtaining benefits for a private party who seeks to obtain them by illicit means.

Nevertheless, the original version of the wording did not include the word "illicitly." This word was added at our suggestion, since without it, any lawful lobbying action would have been included as a potential act of corruption.

The concept could be identified with an instigation to government fraud, except that it does not require that there be harm to state patrimony.

If we consider that the classification of crimes that states might penalize under the model of that commitment applies to a private party and not to a public official, the wording of the regulation should be very precise, because the search for benefits by private individuals is natural, unless they use clearly illegitimate methods.

Despite the inclusion of the word "illicitly," in our view the intended concept is not yet sufficiently clear. There is some doubt as to the objective of the illegality for the act to be considered corrupt. Does the illegality refer to the means or the ends?

The word "illicitly," used as such, i.e., as an adverb of mode, appears to indicate that it refers to means. Otherwise, the formula would say "illicit benefits" rather than "illicitly." However, neither does the wording read "to illicitly seek" but rather "a decision . . . whereby he illicitly obtains." The illegality occurs after the decision and prior to obtaining the benefit or simultaneously therewith.

Thus, the illegality does not appear to be centered on the procedures used by the private party to attain the benefits. As it is drafted, the paragraph does not refer to the use of unlawful means, such as bribery or threats, to obtain a result.

The requirement of illegality that qualifies the benefit in itself, in the paragraph in question, appears to be even more doubtful. For example: would a request made by lawful means, such as a formal petition, through which a private party seeks an unlawful gain, e.g., the donation of a public plaza to his own benefit, fall under paragraph c? Imposing a penalty for a formal petition does not appear to be very logical, although through such a petition, something is being sought that is not proper.

According to its explanation, paragraph c appears to indicate that the illegality required in the stipulation refers more to the procedure through which the benefit was granted, since the sentence mentions illicit acquisition. Such would be the case, for example, of a contract signed in favor of a company and directly awarded by the authorities, under circumstances in which a competitive bid would have been more appropriate. This interpretation, which is the one that most closely corresponds to the concept's literal meaning, still raises an issue: the illegality of the procedure that awarded the benefit should fall more on the official than on private individuals, yet nevertheless, the concept's active subject is private individuals seeking benefits.

The solution does not appear to be fair, unless the reason the authority adopted an improper procedure was to conceal the circumstances that gave rise to its adoption by the private party, in order to deceive the official. And thus we arrive at the historical sense of the wording. That was precisely the case of the Venezuelan bankers, who convinced their country's authorities to provide them certain treatment that they would not have deserved under the true circumstances, which were concealed.

Deviation of the Purpose of the Property

Paragraph d of section 1 is very similar to paragraph b. It also involves an offense that in many countries is known as "misappropriation of public funds."

Although paragraph d, unlike paragraph b, refers to "deviation" of property, rather than to "use," it involves a deviation to one's "own benefit or that of a third party," such that it may be comparable to a use.

Nevertheless, there is a partial but well-defined difference with respect to the ownership of the property in the two cases. Paragraph b refers only to state property. Paragraph d also involves private property entrusted to an official in deposit or administration. This would be the case of a judge who authorized the use of an automobile held in his court because it had been seized during an assault.

Extradition, Assistance, and Cooperation

For purposes of interpreting sections 2 and 3 of article XI, we refer, respectively, to the sections entitled: "Full Functioning of the Agreement" and "Assistance and Cooperation," in the commentary to article VIII.

ARTICLE XII

EFFECT ON STATE PROPERTY

For application of this Convention, it shall not be necessary that acts of corruption harm State property.

Governments must not only protect the state patrimony but must also refrain from causing injustices to those they govern. What is more, the reason why they must protect the public patrimony is justice to those they govern.

Therefore, corruption does not involve merely the deterioration of state funds. It may also cover a very wide range of acts involving using a public position to one's own advantage or to that of a third party, without causing the least reduction to the state patrimony. Requesting or accepting bribes to perform lawful acts that were one's duty to perform in any case, using classified information on commercial securities, and misallocated permits represent only a few examples of corruption that cause no economic harm to the state; at least, not immediately.

What is more, there are states that benefit from certain acts of corruption, such as transnational bribery and the concealment of property or currency.

But justice, fairness, and international fair play require a firm decision to combat such acts, and to take measures against those who engage in them, in a stage of history when, more than ever, global information is the basis for all decisions.

ARTICLE XIII

EXTRADITION

1. This article shall apply to the offenses established by the States Parties in accordance with this Convention.

2. *Each of the offenses to which this article applies shall be deemed to be included as an extraditable offense in any extradition treaty existing between or among the States Parties. The States Parties undertake to include such offenses as extraditable offenses in every extradition treaty to be concluded between or among them.*

3. *If a State Party that makes extradition conditional on the existence of a treaty receives a request for extradition from another State Party with which it does not have an extradition treaty, it may consider this Convention as the legal basis for extradition with respect to any offense to which this article applies.*

4. *States Parties that do not make extradition conditional on the existence of a treaty shall recognize offenses to which this article applies as extraditable offenses between themselves.*

5. *Extradition shall be subject to the conditions provided for by the law of the Requested State or by applicable extradition treaties, including the grounds on which the Requested State may refuse extradition.*

6. *If extradition for an offense to which this article applies is refused solely on the basis of the nationality of the person sought, or because the Requested State deems that it has jurisdiction over the offense, the Requested State shall submit the case to its competent authorities for the purpose of prosecution unless otherwise agreed with the Requesting State, and shall report the final outcome to the Requesting State in due course.*

7. *Subject to the provisions of its domestic law and its extradition treaties, the Requested State may, upon being satisfied that the circumstances so warrant and are urgent, and at the request of the Requesting State, take into custody a person whose extradition is sought and who is present in its territory, or take other appropriate measures to ensure his presence at extradition proceedings.*

Application

The issue of extradition constituted nothing less than the historical origin of the ICAC, since Venezuela's proposal, on which the Inter-American Juridical Committee worked, was based precisely on a commitment to grant extradition for offenses of corruption, even if the accused party attempted to take refuge in the political content of the events.

Section 1, article XIII, states that the ICAC's extradition standards will apply to "offenses established by the States Parties in accordance with this Convention."

It must not be forgotten, in accordance with everything that has been stated up to now, that offenses the states parties may establish, according to the ICAC, may be based on various types of commitments:

1. The acts of corruption described in article VI, section 1, which the states must establish unconditionally

2. The offense of transnational bribery as provided for in article VIII and the offense of illicit enrichment as provided for in article IX, which each state must establish provided that this legislation is not in violation with its constitution and the basic principles of its legal system
3. The offenses corresponding to the acts of "progressive development" of article XI, whose legislation the states parties deemed appropriate and are required to consider
4. Any other acts of corruption that the states parties have established as an offense, in accordance with article VI, section 2

Of course, extradition for the specified offenses will apply in accordance with the general and specific standards relating to this matter (section 5).

Convention and Extradition Treaties

The existence of extradition treaties between the states parties or the lack of such treaties gives rise to various methods of applying the ICAC, which are described in sections 2, 3, and 4 of article XIII.

In the event of a request for extradition from one state party to another, some of the following situations may arise:

1. There is an extradition treaty between the requesting state and the requested state:
    a. The offenses established in accordance with the ICAC will be considered as being included within those treaties (section 2).
    b. The parties undertake to include the offenses in future treaties (section 2).
2. There is no extradition treaty between the requesting state and the requested state:
    a. The state makes extradition conditional upon a treaty: it may apply the ICAC in substitution (section 3).
    b. The state does not make extradition conditional upon a treaty: it must apply the ICAC standards (section 4).
    c. The parties agree to include the offenses in future treaties (section 2).

As may be seen, there is only one case in which a state requested to undertake extradition has the opportunity to freely decide whether the request is in order, according to the ICAC. This is the case of an ICAC state party that makes extradition conditional upon the existence of a treaty, when it receives a request for extradition from another state party, but has no current extradition treaty with the state party (this is the case of section 3). In this situation, the requested state may consider the convention "as the legal basis for extradition with respect to any offense" to which the ICAC applies.

This is a logical recognition of a general principle of a state's law. There are states that only grant extradition to others with which they have the corresponding treaties. There are other states that do not make extradition conditional upon the existence of a treaty.

Thus, if a state, according to the general principles of its legal system, only grants extradition to states with which it is bound by a corresponding treaty, the convention cannot go so far as to commit it to granting extradition to a state with which it has not signed any treaty. But on the other hand, the ICAC offers itself as a tool to that state, if its authorities wish to use it as a legal basis for granting extradition (section 3).

In the other cases, states are required to grant extradition. If there is a treaty, offenses that the requester and the requested party established in accordance with the ICAC must be considered as being included in that treaty, even if they do not explicitly appear in the convention (section 2).

If there is no treaty, but the requested state does not make extradition conditional upon the existence of a treaty, it must grant extradition for all offenses classified as corrupt acts under the ICAC, provided that the requester and the requested party have established those offenses (section 4).

In all cases, states were required to include the offenses listed in the ICAC as cases of extradition between themselves (section 2).

The conflict that could most likely occur with respect to extradition requests that arise under the ICAC will surely be based on a state's omission or delay in analyzing the legislation to which it committed in the convention. Such a conflict would arise if the requested state bases its refusal of extradition on its own omission, because it is not an offense according to its laws. We must not forget that one of the general principles of international law in matters of extradition is that of double incrimination; i.e., the existence of symmetry between the right of the requesting state and that of the requested state, with respect to the offense for which extradition is requested.

If this situation were to occur, the state that is remiss could be subject to an international legal proceeding, but the acts of corruption described in the ICAC cannot be automatically considered as becoming "crime classifications" under positive law, because for this purpose it would be necessary to have a law that imposes a specific penalty for each such act. Section 1, article XIII, itself states that this "article shall apply to the offenses established by the States Parties in accordance with this Convention." Therefore, the ICAC itself admits the need for it to be established in advance.

On the other hand, as we have already noted, the criminal definitions corresponding to the acts of corruption that have been described were included within the extradition treaties, in the form of a list of offenses, at the same time as the ratification of the ICAC.

General Conditions

Section 5 of article XIII states that "extradition shall be subject to the conditions provided for by the law of the Requested State or by applicable extradition treaties, including the grounds on which the Requested State may refuse extradition."

This section notes the possibility that the requested state may refuse extradition, notwithstanding the occurrence of the circumstances in sections 2, 3, and 4 of the same article. Certainly, these conditions cannot consist of requirements that contradict the agreement established in those sections. To offer an extreme example, after the ICAC, neither a treaty nor a law could say that no extraditions will be granted for bribery offenses.

The conditions will more likely correspond to circumstances unrelated to the offense, which in a certain sense, may be referred to as "formal." In general, this will involve demonstrating that the offense has not expired under the statute of limitations, that the classification of crimes exists as such in the legislation of the requesting country and the requested country, that the penalty does not exceed a certain limit—surely linked to the requested state's maximum—and that the request has been properly filed, etc.

There are other conditions for which the requested state may refuse extradition, such as the nationality of the accused party or the jurisdiction of the state that received the request.

There are states that, as a general and—at times—a constitutional principle, refuse to extradite their nationals. The requested state may also refuse extradition because it deems itself as having jurisdiction, under its domestic law or treaties, to try the accused criminal. In this case, the ICAC attempts to avoid impunity through the commitment assumed by the requested state to prosecute the accused party and notify the requesting state of the results. Section 6 makes these possibilities very clear: "If extradition for an offense to which this article applies is refused solely on the basis of the nationality of the person sought, or because the Requested State deems that it has jurisdiction over the offense, the Requested State shall submit the case to its competent authorities for the purpose of prosecution unless otherwise agreed with the Requesting State, and shall report the final outcome to the Requesting State in due course."

The word "solely" in the above paragraph means that if there are other reasons for which extradition has been refused, in addition to nationality and jurisdiction, the requested state will not be required to fulfill the commitments assumed in section 6, except because of those commitments, and notwithstanding, of course, the requested party's obligations by virtue of treaties or its domestic legislation.

As may be seen, the nationality and jurisdiction of the requested state enjoy lower status among the causes for which extradition may be denied, since a state that refuses extradition based on these circumstances cannot later act absolutely freely, by virtue of the ICAC, but rather is required to report.

The convention's position is logical in establishing the aforementioned differences. If extradition is refused due to the absence of double incrimination or as a consequence of expiration under the statute of limitations for the offense, for example, the requested state cannot be required to undertake criminal prosecution of the accused party, precisely because these reasons prohibit such prosecution. On the other hand, if the authorities of the requested state claim that the accused party is a national of that country or claim their own jurisdiction to prosecute the accused criminal, the government of the requesting state is entitled to know whether the defendant has actually been prosecuted or whether the claimed arguments were only excuses to ensure impunity. What is more, the international community is morally interested in knowing these circumstances. The ICAC and treaties lawfully support this moral intent.

Custody

Section 7 of article XIII considers the possibility of the requested state's taking into protective custody an individual whose extradition has been requested by another state party.

The section was drafted with extreme care, since the value at risk is the physical freedom of individuals and therefore the signatories did not wish to assume more commitments than those they already had, in this regard, by virtue of treaties. For this reason, notwithstanding the fact that the section uses a voluntary form—"the Requested State may"—it also stipulates a series of conditions, all of which must be fulfilled prior to taking the individual into custody:

1. The measure must not violate the requested state's domestic legal standards.
2. The measure must not contradict the stipulations of treaties signed by the requested party.
3. The circumstances must justify custody as a means of ensuring the accused party's appearance.
4. The circumstances must justify the urgency of the measure.
5. Of course, there must be a request from another state.

The requested state may also "take other appropriate measures to ensure" the appearance of the accused party "at extradition proceedings." This may involve, for example, collecting bail or taking another precautionary measure.

It must be expected that to the extent the ICAC demonstrates its positive effects and the states adapt to complying with its standards, this article will be updated to make custody mandatory, upon verifying the conditions stipulated in section 7.

ARTICLE XIV

ASSISTANCE AND COOPERATION

In accordance with their domestic laws and applicable treaties, the States Parties shall afford one another the widest measure of mutual assistance by processing requests from authorities that, in conformity with their domestic laws, have the power to investigate or prosecute the acts of corruption described in this Convention, to obtain evidence and take other necessary action to facilitate legal proceedings and measures regarding the investigation or prosecution of acts of corruption.

The States Parties shall also provide each other with the widest measure of mutual technical cooperation on the most effective ways and means of preventing, detecting, investigating and punishing acts of corruption. To that end, they shall foster exchanges of experiences by way of agreements and meetings between competent bodies and institutions, and shall pay special attention to methods and procedures of citizen participation in the fight against corruption.

Widest Measure of Assistance

Article XIV is one of the ICAC's innovative solutions in contributing to the fight against corruption. The novelty consists in the scope of assistance and cooperation, which is not limited to requests and judicial responses but rather makes possible communication between administrative bodies of the states parties. This scope is fundamental for detecting and punishing offenses.

The original article, according to the wording of the Inter-American Juridical Committee, consisted only of the first paragraph, and according to the most typical solution, provided only for assistance and cooperation between judges. That article said literally and exclusively the following: "In accordance with their domestic laws and applicable treaties, the States Parties shall afford one another the widest measure of mutual assistance, to obtain evidence and take other necessary action to facilitate legal proceedings and measures regarding acts of corruption in public functions."

This means that if one state requires information from another state, to obtain information on an offense, a judge must request such information, and in general, another judge must order that reports be submitted, although according to law this may also be ordered by another authority.

However, the problem of exclusively legal cooperation does not correspond to the state that must provide the information, but rather to the state that must request it.

If it is required that a request for information be made solely by a judge, one must assume the existence of an open legal case, which is the reason for the intervention of a criminal judge in requesting the reports. But a criminal legal case is opened when there is an accusation—by a private individual or an official—through which information is offered as to the possible commission of an offense. However, it is precisely that minimum necessary information needed to make an accusation that may be in another country and, therefore, concealed from the view of likely accusers.

This case is a vicious circle, which occurs rather frequently: Lack of information because there is no judge to request it. There is no judge to request such information because there is no open criminal case resulting in the assignment of a judge. There is no open criminal case because there is no accusation. There is no accusation because there is no information to justify it. This is the argument we brought up during the Washington negotiations, which was condensed into a proposal by the Argentine delegation to eliminate the word "legal" as well as "legal proceedings and measures," to make possible a prior administrative investigation. Specifically, the Argentine delegation proposed that the authority to request reports be extended to the administrative authorities in a wide sense.

After certain objections from the Uruguayan delegation, which supported keeping exclusively legal assistance as a means of preserving some personal guarantees, e.g., the right to privacy, the Argentine delegation, along with those of Peru and Venezuela, among other countries that supported the innovation, proposed a consensus draft that would limit the power to request information to "authorities that, in conformity with their domestic laws, have the power to investigate or prosecute acts of corruption."

Nor did two other proposals from Uruguay, directed at restricting assistance and cooperation for reasons of public order, succeed. One of them read: "The Requested State will be able to consider itself as not required to offer the requested cooperation when it has sufficient grounds to believe that such assistance would clearly violate essential standards or principles of the public order."

The other raised the following principles: sovereignty, security, the public order, "or other fundamental interests."

Although the proposing parties noted, with laudable legal reasoning, similar precedents from the United Nations Convention against Illicit Traffic in Narcotic Drugs (article 7) and the Inter-American Convention on Mutual Assistance in Criminal Matters (article 9), it was not possible, in our view, to yield to the precedent at this time. The ICAC's greatest value lies precisely in the limits that governments impose on themselves with regard to a matter that may otherwise be sensitive: corruption. If the governments themselves could do away with those limits by invoking the public order, basic interests, or other concepts of potentially elastic scope, the entire convention would be subject to the risk of collapse.

The ICAC cannot be interpreted if one does not address its truly innovative nature with respect to its international precedents and the domestic law of countries. It is a new instrument for a new stage of the law of nations.

The solution arrived at is fair, it addresses the fears relating to the possibility of arbitrary or indiscriminate requests, but it retains a great deal of flexibility. Requests for reports cannot be made by just any legal or administrative authority, but rather by those authorized to undertake the investigation or prosecute acts of corruption. The "or," as a copulative conjunction, indicates that agencies with the authority to undertake the investigation (which includes prevention) may make the request, even if they are not responsible for prosecuting the alleged offense.

The aforementioned formula allows auditors and the oversight authorities, such as comptrollers, auditors, customs, intelligence agencies or antidrug agencies, central banks, inspectors general, tax agencies, government ethics offices, domestic affairs offices, trustees of state companies, police, etc., to be authorized to request information from another state party, which may also respond to those reports without the intervention of its judges.

Naturally, the method on which those communications are based will be the one provided for in article XVIII, but this procedure is merely formal and does not constitute an obstacle to the investigation.

The scope of this formula extends to measures on property (article XV) and to the requirements for assistance with respect to bank accounts in another state party (article XVI), which form part of the item regulated by article XIV, although in those two cases, domestic law may set some limits that do not invalidate the purposes of the convention, as we shall see in the respective commentaries.

Thus, the transparency that occurs as a consequence of administrative decentralization increases through the decentralization of corruption investigations.

Technical Cooperation

The second innovation with respect to the original wording of article XIV is the stipulation on technical cooperation, which corresponds to an excellent proposal from the Peruvian delegation in which the U.S. delegation actively cooperated.

Through that clause, "the States Parties shall also provide each other with the widest measure of mutual technical cooperation on the most effective ways and means of preventing, detecting, investigating and punishing acts of corruption."

At a time when technology is progressing daily, it is extremely important that the government's success in discovering effective methods of fighting corruption be communicated to others, who may thereby benefit from such experiences. Inter-American solidarity thus will accelerate legal security on the continent.

The innumerable forms and methods intended to form part of the technical cooperation may include intelligence strategies, electronic or digital technology, computer programs, proposed agencies and laws, legal and administrative procedures, statistics, etc.

The Organization of American States may develop an extraordinarily useful database for supporting this provision.

But it is also important that governments and international agencies support nongovernmental organizations in this task, as they are active agents in the transformation of systems and may even, at times, promote those changes faster than the states themselves, thanks to the lack of excessively bureaucratic structures.

Indeed, the second part of the formula provides that states "shall foster exchanges of experience by way of agreements and meetings between competent bodies and institutions, and shall pay special attention to methods and procedures of citizen participation in the fight against corruption."

Civil society organizations not only can promote exchanges of experiences with similar institutions and governments of other countries, but also can participate actively in the fight against corruption. This active participation may be applied by exercising the rights of information and petition that citizens have in any free state, through which they may monitor the actions of their government. At the same time, nongovernmental organizations tend to promote laws that increase administrative transparency in their own countries, with a view to facilitating such monitoring.

ARTICLE XV

MEASURES REGARDING PROPERTIES

In accordance with their applicable domestic laws and relevant treaties or other agreements that may be in force between or among them, the States Parties shall provide each other the widest possible measure of assistance in the identification, tracing, freezing, seizure and forfeiture of property or proceeds obtained, derived from or used in the commission of offenses established in accordance with this Convention.

A State Party that enforces its own or another State Party's forfeiture judgment against property or proceeds described in paragraph 1 of this article shall dispose of the property or proceeds in accordance with its laws. To the extent permitted by a State Party's laws and upon such terms as it deems appropriate, it may transfer all or part of such property or proceeds to another State Party that assisted in the underlying investigation or proceedings.

Property "Obtained," "Derived from," or "Used"

The assistance provided for in article XIV extends, as we mentioned in its commentary, to cooperation between the states parties for adopting certain measures on "property ... obtained [or] derived from ... the commission of offenses" to which the convention refers. Also included in the provision is property "used" in committing an offense or the "proceeds" of such property.

Offenses taken into consideration with respect to such property are, as indicated in the article itself, those "established in accordance with this Convention," a reference that includes the acts covered by article VI, sections 1 and 2, and articles VIII, IX, and XI.

As a standard of interpretation for identifying the property involved, paragraph three of article I must be taken into consideration, which refers to "assets of any kind, whether movable or immovable, tangible or intangible, and any document or legal instrument demonstrating, purporting to demonstrate, or relating to ownership or other rights pertaining to such assets."

In summary, the obligation of assistance with respect to property covers:

1. Property obtained in committing an offense. Property that has been obtained by public officials or third parties involved as a consequence of the commission of the offense. For example, money or objects delivered as a bribe.
2. Property deriving from such acts. This property consists of the proceeds acquired with the money originating from an offense, or the exchange of such property or its investment in legal or illegal businesses.
3. The property used in committing such an offense. In all cases, but particularly in this one, one must consider that the word "commission" is to be understood in its wide sense. It is not only the principal offense, but also participation, concealment, instigation, etc. Therefore, any property used in any such acts is included within article XV. As an example of the scope of this clause, it might be claimed that if the computer was used when arranging a transnational bribe, to transmit data or electronic mail, that computer and its data files might be subject to the provisions of article XV. Certainly, in all cases, the stipulations of article I, paragraph 3, must be taken into consideration.
4. The proceeds of the property obtained or used. Paragraph 1 of article XV refers to the "proceeds" of such property. There is therefore no distinction between property "obtained," "derived from," or "used" and consequently, the proceeds are the economic results of any of those categories of property.

Scope, Domestic Law, and Treaties

Article XV provides for "the widest possible measure of assistance." This case also omits all reference to legal assistance. Therefore, property-related assistance—which, in the end, is assistance—is what is provided for in article XIV, with all its consequences.

The reference to domestic legislation, as mentioned at the beginning of the article, classifies the procedure for assistance from the requested state and the institutions of that state that may take certain measures. The laws of a state may, for example, provide that an attachment may only be applied by a judge of the requested state, but they may not restrict the scope of the agreed-upon assistance.

The reference to treaties, in the same location, shows the need for an absence of conflict between the ICAC and current agreements between the requesting state and the requested state.

This safeguard must be interpreted in a flexible sense, in favor of facilitating investigation. If there is no explicit opposition—which does not mean a mere difference—between the convention and treaties, the requested state must provide the widest possible measure of assistance, because this is the spirit and even the letter of the commitment that has been engaged.

Identification, Tracing, Freezing, Seizure, and Forfeiture

When interpreting the actions stipulated for assistance with respect to property, differences in language and expressions between the states parties must be taken into consideration, which makes necessary a range of appropriate terms so as not to leave any action outside of the commitment.

"Identification," in this case, as the word itself indicates, means to establish the identity of a thing with respect to that which is being sought.

"Tracing" is the act of searching itself, and although this term received various objections during the Washington meetings, it was the one that ended up being adopted, since it was the one that came closest to all parties' ideas relating to this type of procedure.

"Freezing" is a typical precautionary measure intended to prevent the disappearance or transfer of an asset subject to investigation. It must not be interpreted solely in the physical sense. An attachment or a restriction intended to prevent a party from transferring property is a form of freezing.

"Seizure," which in many countries is classified as a penalty, and in this sense tends to be unconstitutional, must be interpreted as being the legal dispossession of a property owned by the accused party in reparation for the effects of an offense, and in this sense, it is absolutely lawful.

"Forfeiture," according to the language of almost all the countries, is the dispossession of the effects used in committing the offense or property obtained through the offense.

In any event, the list of possible actions is not exhaustive, and in any case, all requests are covered by the widest possible measure of assistance and co-operation under article XIV.

Distribution of Property

The second paragraph of article XV, which was proposed by the United States, corresponds to a formula of the United Nations drug trafficking convention (Vienna Convention), pursuant to which a state that has cooperated in an investigation on an act of corruption, at the request of another state party, may benefit from the distribution of a portion of the property forfeited as a result of the offense, provided that this distribution is lawful.

Nevertheless, the first part of paragraph two of article XV reads "a State Party that enforces its own or another State Party's forfeiture judgment against property or proceeds described in paragraph 1 of this article shall dispose of the property or proceeds in accordance with its laws."

This is a logical provision, since this forfeited property is precisely that which is on the territory of the state executing the ruling and that is the reason for its intervention. In this text, the possibility of distributing the property, which falls within the authority of that state, provides for submitting to the domestic legitimacy of such distribution and to prudent assessment by the corresponding authorities. This is the text of the final part of the paragraph, which states, "To the extent permitted by a State Party's laws and upon such terms as it deems appropriate, it may transfer all or part of such property or proceeds to another State Party that assisted in the underlying investigation or proceedings."

Notwithstanding the clarity of the language, the word "underlying" could raise some questions as to the scope of the clause. Does the benefit correspond only to legal proceedings oriented toward property, or may it extend, for example, to legal extradition procedures? The location of the paragraph, within an article dedicated solely to measures relating to property, appears to indicate that extradition would be excluded. Nevertheless, an underlying legal proceeding, in this case, is one precisely because it is not necessarily subordinate to the requirements on property but rather is able to maintain a collateral relationship with respect to those requirements.

Certainly, customs and styles will play a fundamental role in these cases, and in the end, the distribution of property is voluntary for the state that performs it, such that any interpretations of the intended scope are theoretical from the standpoint of international law. However, the interpretation of this standard will have domestic importance to a government that proposes to distribute this forfeited property, because the degree of freedom that the authorities have to perform such distribution will depend upon this interpretation.

ARTICLE XVI

BANK SECRECY

The Requested State shall not invoke bank secrecy as a basis for refusal to provide the assistance sought by the Requesting State. The Requested State shall apply this article in accordance with its domestic law, its procedural provisions, or bilateral or multilateral agreements with the Requesting State.

The Requesting State shall be obligated not to use any information received that is protected by bank secrecy for any purpose other than the proceeding for which that information was requested, unless authorized by the Requested State.

Absolute Impossibility of Claiming Secrecy

The impossibility of claiming bank secrecy in the face of requests for assistance from an authority of another state, within the context of an investigation on corruption, is one of the most important clauses of the ICAC.

This provision appeared in the draft by the Inter-American Juridical Committee and was later promoted by a proposal of the United States. However, the final wording of the first paragraph corresponds to a consensus proposal from Mexico.

At the time of the Washington discussions, the Argentine delegation opposed any condition that might reduce the scope of the assistance the states are required to provide, but we believe that the solution that was arrived at, thanks to the Mexican proposal, is reasonable and sufficient for the convention's purposes.

First, we should note that the assistance that the requested state should offer by virtue of this clause is the wide measure of assistance of article XIV. It does not involve any other type of assistance. Article XVI only adds to that obligation the nonexceptionable nature of bank secrecy in the face of a request. This means that a state may request assistance through any "authorities that, in conformity with their domestic laws, have the power to investigate or prosecute the acts of corruption." Therefore, it is not necessary for it be a judge who requests reports on a bank account. In this regard, we refer to everything that has been stated in the commentaries to article XIV (Widest Measures of Assistance).

As may be seen, the impossibility of claiming bank secrecy is final and absolute: the article reads, "shall not invoke bank secrecy as a basis for refusal to provide the assistance sought by the Requesting State." However, it may be assumed that the second part of the paragraph makes that obligation relative insofar as it stipulates: "The Requested State shall apply this article in accordance with its domestic law, its procedural provisions, or bilateral or multilateral agreements with the Requesting State."

Above all, it must be taken into consideration that this provision cannot be interpreted separately from the above, which is absolute: "shall not invoke bank secrecy as a basis for refusal to provide the assistance." Thus, any stipulation that succeeds this clause must be understood in its relationship to the forms and not to the core of the article, which cannot be distorted.

This interpretation is confirmed by the very beginning of the second part of the paragraph: "The Requested State shall apply this article." The article refers solely to the impossibility of claiming bank secrecy. How could it be applied if the provisions subordinate to that purpose completely canceled it? That would be a contradiction. If the text had been included in article XIV on assistance and cooperation in general, it might—perhaps—have raised some doubts. But the mandate "shall apply," which is also categorical, was included within the article on bank secrecy. There is no other purpose to the article, outside of the impossibility of claiming that secrecy. The subsequent specific items in the commitment are only provisions subordinate to the principal purpose.

There is therefore no way of determining how an article can be applied or not applied at the same time; that is, that it be applied in accordance with domestic legal standards that require it not to be applied.

In conclusion, the standards of the Vienna Convention on the Law of Treaties must be noted, articles 26 and 31 of which recognize that treaties must be fulfilled in good faith, and article 27 of which provides that "a party may not invoke the provisions of its internal law as justification for its failure to perform a treaty."

Subordinate Standards

After establishing the absolute nature of the commitment to offer assistance without being able to claim bank secrecy, it is necessary to interpret the meaning of the provision subordinate to that obligation: "in accordance with its domestic law, its procedural provisions, or bilateral or multilateral agreements with the Requesting State."

The part that raises the most doubts in the aforementioned phrase is the reference to domestic law, since there then follows the need to adapt the method of the response to the provisions of the requested state's procedure. Is this a redundancy or, in fact, is domestic law consistent with providing assistance? Neither.

We have already established the subordinate nature of all these conditions with respect to the principal commitment: not to claim bank secrecy as a basis for denying assistance.

But neither must the reference to domestic law be identified with procedural standards. There may be numerous standards that require certain conditions for fulfillment and that do not strictly consist in procedural standards. Thus, for example, if the domestic law of the requested state provides that the data from a bank account may only be supplied at the order of a judge, the central authority of that state (article XVIII) will pass the request on to a judge with jurisdiction over the requested institution. But on the other hand, domestic law may not set conditions to which the requesting state must be subject, the only standard of which is, in this case, the ICAC.

The procedure, on the other hand, will indicate the methods for processing that request: the forms, deadlines, data to be provided, etc.

Finally, treaties are also subordinate to fulfillment of the commitment to offer assistance, because the ICAC, for the domestic order of each country insofar as it concerns current treaties, is a subsequent standard, which prevails over prior standards.

Limited Use

Paragraph two of article XVI contains a limitation on the requesting state, which "shall be obligated not to use any information received that is protected by bank secrecy for any purpose other than the proceeding for which that information was requested, unless authorized by the Requested State."

According to this stipulation, the requesting state could not, for example, after obtaining the necessary information for a bribery or illicit enrichment investigation, use that same data for a tax prosecution.

Although we do not share this ambivalence as to the effects of the truth, which generally protect, at the least, harm caused by one party to another party—an individual or a legal entity—we believe that the clause may be understandable at this stage. Too much progress has been achieved as to risk rejection by a significant number of countries, because of an extreme initial requirement.

At the same time, we must trust in the likelihood that the requested states will authorize the unconditional use of information, in light of an international order that is demanding increasing transparency from its participants.

ARTICLE XVII

NATURE OF ACT

For the purposes of articles XIII, XIV, XV and XVI of this Convention, the fact that the property obtained or derived from an act of corruption was intended

*for political purposes, or that it is alleged that an act of corruption was com-
mitted for political motives or purposes, shall not suffice in and of itself to
qualify the act as a political offense or as a common offense related to a political offense.*

Insignificance of the Purpose of Corrupt Acts

The wording of article XVII, notwithstanding its novelty as a contribution,
was one of the first ones created within the ICAC. Its central idea, which is
the need to disassociate corruption from politics, was the core of the
Venezuela plan. The original Venezuelan proposal even absolutely rejected
the possibility of asylum with regard to acts of corruption.

The Inter-American Juridical Committee and subsequent proposals, in view
of the constitutionality of the right of asylum claimed by many countries,
amended the wording and leaned toward a formula that we might refer to here
as "the insignificance of the use of property obtained through an act of corruption." Subsequently, in the work of the Inter-American Juridical Committee, the
well-reasoned vote of Dr. Alberto Zelada Castedo, supported by a motion from
the Argentine Foreign Ministry, gave the article its current form.

On that occasion, Dr. Zelada Castedo proposed adding to the idea of insufficiency of political intent of corrupt acts, insufficiency of the allegation of such
purpose or intent, for purposes of establishing the political nature of the act.

This formula will apply, in most cases, to prevent government officials,
who are precisely the ones who can engage in acts of corruption, from evad-
ing their responsibility by invoking the political nature of their acts. Unfortunately, in the Americas there are shameful examples of officials who, after
their enrichment, end up playing the role of victims in a political prosecution,
and through such a farce, can calmly enjoy the proceeds of their offenses.

Because of the sad history of events such as the one described above, due to
which many officials obtain political asylum in other countries, at a certain
stage of the work of the meeting of experts this clause was included in the chapter on extradition. Nevertheless, it was more appropriately applied to relate this
principle to the functioning of the entire convention, insofar as it applies.

As may be clearly seen in the wording of the article, the political use of the
property or the claim of political motivation or purpose will not prevent application of the clauses on extradition, assistance and cooperation, and the
measures on property and on lifting bank secrecy.

An Issue to Reflect Upon

The category "political act" has very deep roots in international law, due,
among other reasons, to the political persecution that many individuals truly
suffer throughout the world.

If we take that fact into account, we must admit that the form of the ICAC is an extremely important step forward in the legal relationships between the peoples of the Americas.

However, perhaps at a more advanced stage of the evolution of international law, it will be necessary to focus on certain "cracks" that, in our judgment, were left open by article XVII.

The clause focuses almost exclusively on public officials who benefit economically from a corrupt act, and in this sense, covers almost the entire range of cases that might arise. But its wording, at a minimum, raises certain doubts that should be analyzed in the future.

According to the ICAC, there is a series of circumstances that "shall not suffice in and of itself to qualify the act as a political offense or as a common offense related to a political offense." These circumstances are the following:

1. The political use of the property obtained through an act of corruption
2. The allegation of political motivation for the corrupt act
3. The allegation of the political purpose of the corrupt act

However, article XVII states that the circumstances "shall not suffice in and of [themselves]."

But what would happen if such circumstances were accompanied by others, or by evidence?

We believe that it is the very category of "political offense" that deserves an exhaustive analysis, the existence of which is being called into legal question, in light of the ICAC.

ARTICLE XVIII

CENTRAL AUTHORITIES

For the purposes of international assistance and cooperation provided under this Convention, each State Party may designate a central authority or may rely upon such central authorities as are provided for in any relevant treaties or other agreements.

The central authorities shall be responsible for making and receiving the requests for assistance and cooperation referred to in this Convention.

The central authorities shall communicate with each other directly for the purposes of this Convention.

This article is a clause that is very easy to interpret. All agreements of this nature require that each country have a body that consolidates all requests arriving from other states parties, to distribute them within its government or decide whether such requests are improper, as well as to forward requests from their legal or administrative bodies. This is necessary for reasons of order, seriousness, fairness, and sovereignty.

The existence of a central authority prevents anarchy in the country's communications with the outside, lends greater seriousness to requests and responses, provides a guarantee of fairness with respect to the consistency of the responses the state offers to various requests, and addresses the right and obligation of the central government with respect to handling outside relations.

In general, the central authorities are the foreign ministries of each country, but in this case, they could be the justice ministries or departments. However, foreign ministries have the advantage of familiarity with diplomatic language, international experience, and greater knowledge of the true situation facing their interlocutor.

ARTICLE XIX

TEMPORAL APPLICATION

Subject to the constitutional principles and the domestic laws of each State and existing treaties between the States Parties, the fact that the alleged act of corruption was committed before this Convention entered into force shall not preclude procedural cooperation in criminal matters between the States Parties. This provision shall in no case affect the principle of non-retroactivity in criminal law, nor shall application of this provision interrupt existing statutes of limitations relating to crimes committed prior to the date of the entry into force of this Convention.

Retroactivity or Cooperation on Prior Events?

Article XIX arose as a consequence of the joint proposal by Peru and Colombia, supported by the United States, which was aimed at facilitating full application of the ICAC with respect to events occurring prior to its entry into force. The Peruvian delegation argued that this decision was legitimately possible because it was not the application of a retroactive criminal law but rather of cooperation between states to make possible the application of criminal laws prior to any offenses.

The proposal was tempting, and addressed the spirit of all parties concerned regarding the need to avoid even the slightest degree of impunity. At the same time, certain fears arose with regard to the clause's possible indirect impact on the principle of nonretroactivity of the criminal law.

Between the prospect of making the ICAC applicable to all cases, with no restrictions based on the time an act occurred, and the possibility—sketched out by certain country representatives—of preventing any application of the convention to offenses occurring prior to its entry into force, a formula was suggested by the Argentine delegation to avoid the protection of impunity, without harming constitutional guarantees.

Application Conditions

The formula that was developed to resolve the difference that had arisen as a result of the temporal application of the ICAC is simpler than it might seem at first glance.

First, a condition was included similar to the one preceding the articles on transnational bribery and illicit enrichment, although somewhat wider in scope.

Second, the possibility was explicitly raised of offering criminal procedural cooperation for events prior to the convention's entry into force.

Finally, those circumstances that raised fears because of the possible violation of the principle of legality were explicitly left untouched. It was agreed then that the clause shall "in no case affect the principle of non-retroactivity in criminal law, nor shall application of this provision interrupt existing statutes of limitations relating to crimes committed prior to the date of the entry into force of this Convention."

Therefore, the conditions for offering international cooperation on acts prior to the ICAC are the following:

1. The lack of conflict between the act of cooperation and the constitutional principles of the requested state.
2. The lack of conflict between the act of cooperation and the legal standards of the requested state.
3. The lack of conflict between the act of cooperation and treaties binding the requesting state to the requested state. The conflict in this case, as in points 1 and 2, must be explicit, and it is not sufficient to claim that the treaty or the standard does not take into consideration the solution being sought. To prevent cooperation, this act must be in direct conflict with one of the provisions introduced as safeguards.
4. The appropriateness of the requests, in accordance with the ICAC's general clauses.
5. Compatibility between cooperation and respect for the criminal law's non-retroactivity; such that, to raise an extreme example, if a request were based on the intent to apply a criminal law of the requesting state that was

decreed pursuant to the ICAC but which did not exist prior to it, cooperation would not be feasible.

6. Cooperation will not interrupt the statute of limitations in effect for offenses
committed prior to the convention.

The stipulation mentioned above in point 6 is the one that may raise the
greatest concern with regard to any requests for cooperation, including the
possibility of extradition.

The error that an interpreter of this clause could most easily fall into is most
likely to assume that it is possible to refuse cooperation whenever, according
to the law of the requesting state, it is suitable for interrupting the statute of
limitations for an offense committed before the convention entered into force.
Such an interpretation would not take into account the fact that a state that ratifies the ICAC has also acquired a legal obligation.

Simply put, cooperation must be provided, but the act of cooperation will
not be used to suspend the statute of limitations for the offense in the requesting state.

The ICAC becomes the law for states that ratify it. In every country, subsequent law and specific law revoke prior law and general law, respectively,
in cases of conflict. The provision of article XIX, insofar as it provides that
the criminal procedural cooperation that is provided will not suspend the
statute of limitations, is a law subsequent to the general standards of the requesting state's statute of limitations. Therefore, those general standards on
the statute of limitations, upon ratification of the convention, are amended in
such a way as to not apply to the specific cases provided for in article XIX of
the ICAC. This means that criminal procedural cooperation offered for offenses prior to the convention's entry into force will not be capable of sus-
pending the statute of limitations for these offenses in the requesting state.

This is the sense of the provision: "nor shall application of this provision
interrupt," which assumes, in itself, that there is an application.

Consequently, if one state party requests that another state party extradite an
accused party, solely by virtue of this ICAC and for an offense committed
prior to the document's entry into force, the requested state must grant the
extradition—if the general conditions are fulfilled—but the statute of limitations for the accused party's offense will continue to run as if the extradition
had not occurred. The requesting state must therefore pardon or convict the accused party within the statute of limitations period, calculated as from the date
the alleged act was committed, or as from the final suspension prior to
the requests for extradition, the application of the convention notwithstanding.

However, any discussion could be moot for states that consider the statute
of limitations as suspended upon a mere request for cooperation, even if the

request is inoperable, since a request is indicative of a willingness to further the proceeding. Since such a request would be prior to the application of the clause, it could be interpreted as interrupting the statute of limitations.

ARTICLE XX

OTHER AGREEMENTS OR PRACTICES

No provision of this Convention shall be construed as preventing the States Parties from engaging in mutual cooperation within the framework of other international agreements, bilateral or multilateral, currently in force or concluded in the future, or pursuant to any other applicable arrangement or practice.

Simply put, article XX acknowledges the need to preserve the widest degree of latitude and applicability of international law.

The ICAC seeks to expand the system of standards directed at preventing, detecting, and punishing corruption. If there are other agreements or practices aimed at the same purpose that include solutions of greater scope than those of the Caracas agreement, it is not the convention itself that will prevent the exercise of those possibilities.

ARTICLE XXI

SIGNATURE

This Convention is open for signature by the Member States of the Organization of American States.

The ICAC was signed within the framework of the Organization of American States, and it is therefore open to the signatures of the states comprising the OAS.

Signing of the convention implies the desire to join as a party to the agreement.

Twenty-one states signed the convention on March 26, 1996, in Caracas; an unusually high number for an agreement with such wide consequences and deep commitments. Other states did not sign the act, due to the need to first undertake formal legal procedures or because of the need to examine the political timeliness of doing so.

But the enthusiasm demonstrated in Caracas is the best sign of the consensus received by this instrument, not only by the governments, but also by the people whose interests they administer.

ARTICLE XXII

RATIFICATION

This Convention is subject to ratification. The instruments of ratification shall be deposited with the General Secretariat of the Organization of American States.

Like any international agreement, the ICAC is subject to ratification by the congresses or legislative branches of the signatory countries, depending upon the constitutional or legal procedures that each state party has for accomplishing this.

The ratification instruments must be deposited with the General Secretariat of the Organization of American States, because this is the method used by the international agency and the other states to determine whether a state has ratified the document.

Merely by making this deposit, a state becomes a party to the convention, notwithstanding the immediate application of some ratified standards, even prior to the filing of the instrument, in accordance with each state party's constitution and legislation.

ARTICLE XXIII

ACCESSION

This Convention shall remain open for accession by any other State. The instruments of accession shall be deposited with the General Secretariat of the Organization of American States.

Accession by other states parties that are not members of the OAS is an adequate and political invitation to the combat, which will only be sufficiently effective when it becomes intercontinental in scope.

At the time of this edition, certain ideas aimed at similar negotiations in the "Old World" were taking shape in Europe.

For its part, in May 1994 the Organization for Economic Cooperation and Development, which is based in Paris, urged its members to punish transnational bribery and invited other states to do the same.

The United Nations also issued a document on this subject, although it is currently only a declaration.

ARTICLE XXIV

RESERVATION

The States Parties may, at the time of adoption, signature, ratification, or accession, make reservations to this Convention, provided that each reservation concerns one or more specific provisions and is not incompatible with the object and purpose of the Convention.

The article identifies the stages when a state may make reservations to this ICAC. Such reservations must not be inconsistent with the object and purpose of the document and must apply to one or more specific provisions.

Although the possibility of reservations is a standard clause, it is not easy to imagine what reservations might be made without being inconsistent with the object and purpose of the convention.

If it were the clauses that might raise problems of constitutionality from the standpoint of any state party, a reservation is not necessary because in those cases safeguards have already been introduced to allow full ratification of the document without assuming the allegedly unconstitutional obligation.

ARTICLE XXV

ENTRY INTO FORCE

This Convention shall enter into force on the thirtieth day following the date of deposit of the second instrument of ratification. For each State ratifying or acceding to the Convention after the deposit of the second instrument of ratification, the Convention shall enter into force on the thirtieth day after deposit by such State of its instrument of ratification or accession.

As may be seen, an appropriate formula has been established for the speedy entry into force of the convention, which is the deposit of only two states' ratifications. This has already occurred, and the first two states that filed their ratification and implemented the ICAC were Paraguay and Bolivia.

In all cases, a thirty-day period was established for the entry into force, which is necessary to fulfill formal communications requirements but which, at the same time, serves the purpose of avoiding the undesired consequences of a premature entry into the system.

ARTICLE XXVI

DENUNCIATION

This Convention shall remain in force indefinitely, but any of the States Parties may denounce it. The instrument of denunciation shall be deposited with the General Secretariat of the Organization of American States. One year from the date of deposit of the instrument of denunciation, the Convention shall cease to be in force for the denouncing State, but shall remain in force for the other States Parties.

The above article contains three fundamental principles:

1. The indefinite duration of the ICAC
2. The possibility afforded to any state of denouncing the document
3. The need for the passage of a reasonable period of time for the convention to no longer be in force

It would not be logical for an agreement with such high purposes to be limited by time; consequently, the ICAC's indefinite duration is absolutely consistent with its purposes and content.

The possibility of denouncing the agreement; i.e., of withdrawing from the system established by the convention, is a current standard in international law and is based on the sovereign power of states to bind themselves or cease to bind themselves with other states, with a view to the purposes set by their governments.

At the same time, we must avoid the possibility of using such a measure to avoid an imminent commitment, for reasons of circumstances of the moment. It is for this reason that the ICAC sets a waiting period of one year between the denunciation date and date the agreement ceases to be in force.

ARTICLE XXVII

ADDITIONAL PROTOCOLS

Any State Party may submit for the consideration of other States Parties meeting at a General Assembly of the Organization of American States draft additional protocols to this Convention to contribute to the attainment of the purposes set forth in Article II thereof. Each additional protocol shall establish the terms for its entry into force and shall apply only to those States that become Parties to it.

Article XXVII is a clause that is extremely useful to the convention and its purposes. Although it is obvious that the states parties may expand the clauses of the ICAC by a majority decision, it is appropriate to explicitly consider the possibility of doing so through an already established mechanism: submitting additional protocols on the occasions provided for by the General Assembly of the Organization of American States.

During the course of analyzing the convention, we have seen numerous provisions that do not yet have binding force. The possibility of having a flexible mechanism for expansion will allow conversion of the recommendations into explicitly mandatory clauses, to the extent that historical circumstances make it desirable. Experience with exercising commitments will also make it possible to determine which inclusions the document requires for it to best function.

It must also be agreed that the fight against corruption is a road with no temporal end, which therefore requires that strategies oriented toward that purpose be continually refined. Just as the states perfect their instruments for combating crime, so too organized crime, and even contingent delinquency, perfect their tactics to achieve impunity.

We could ask for nothing better than a dynamic convention, with flexible authority to promote ongoing expansion or adaptation within the scope of international law.

ARTICLE XXVIII

DEPOSIT OF ORIGINAL INSTRUMENT

The original instrument of this Convention, the English, French, Portuguese, and Spanish texts of which are equally authentic, shall be deposited with the General Secretariat of the Organization of American States, which shall forward an authenticated copy of its text to the Secretariat of the United Nations for registration and publication in accordance with Article 102 of the United Nations Charter. The General Secretariat of the Organization of American States shall notify its Member States and the States that have acceded to the Convention of signatures, of the deposit of instruments of ratification, accession, or denunciation, and of reservations, if any.

Article XXVIII is practically standard and describes the current procedure for registration of the document, ratification, accession and denunciation, and their communication to the states parties. This is a necessary mechanism in order for each state to be able to know what it can demand of another in terms of cooperation, in accordance with the ICAC.

It also notes the authenticity of the instruments in the four languages spoken in the countries of America: Spanish, French, English, and Portuguese, the texts of which were reviewed and adapted within the style committee, with representatives of each of those languages.

As an anecdote, we might add that the style committee had only one night, that of March 28, 1996, to complete this task before the signing of the document by the representatives of twenty-one states, which took place on the morning of March 29, in Caracas.

Chapter Three

Conclusions

Is the Convention Innovative?

There are individuals in various countries who ask whether the ICAC really made any contribution to positive law and if a convention was truly necessary.

We believe we answered the final question in the introduction, when we explained—from our point of view—the reasons why it is appropriate to combat corruption internationally. Even had the ICAC not contributed a single new item to the existing law, it would have played an extremely important role in establishing a network of international solidarity intended to strengthen and facilitate fulfillment of that law.

But the facts show that the ICAC made new, and possibly even daring, contributions to positive law and international law, in being the first such instrument ever approved.

1. It establishes the obligation of broad assistance and cooperation between states, not subject to requests from judges, to make it possible to seek information before opening a case and thereby allow criminal denunciations to be investigated and prepared without reasonable risk of a lack of evidence.
2. To the same extent, it requires the lifting of bank secrecy with respect to requests for assistance or cooperation carried out within the context of a corruption investigation.
3. It establishes the uselessness of claiming political intent, purpose, or motivation to prevent a request for assistance and cooperation or a request for extradition.
4. It provides support for penalties for the offenses of transnational bribery and illicit enrichment, which are innovative for most national legal systems.

5. It introduces unprecedented preventive measures for a convention, with multiple effects for the administrative law of the member states, including asset declarations by officials and protection for informers of acts of corruption.
6. It extends the notion of "public official" to state servants who have been appointed or elected, even if they have not yet taken office.
7. It promotes activity by civil society and nongovernmental organizations.
8. It provides for the obligation to offer technical assistance on means and methods of preventing, detecting, investigating, and penalizing acts of corruption.
9. It creates systems for extradition, forfeiture, and distribution of seized property, which, although not absolutely innovative, are the most advanced models to date.
10. Finally, as a summary of the entire context, for the first time international action is being taken to prevent, detect, and penalize corruption.

The Principles of the Convention

International law, which is, in the end, "the law of the people," is by its very nature as close to positive law as it is to natural law, from which it directly takes its standards.

Indeed, it is the discipline of international law that extends beyond local ordinances to seek express and programmatic acknowledgment of the principles common to all people, the violation of which aggravates the community of nations. Violations of human rights in general, genocide, terrorism, drug trafficking, and now corruption are some of the evils that have merited international interest.

The text of the convention includes certain moral principles that give meaning to domestic laws and to the interpretation of treaties, without need for exhaustive additional regulation. Institutional legitimacy, moral order and justice, correction, honor, adaptation, integrity, fairness, and efficiency are some of the most visible ones contained in the ICAC. All of them are also consistent with the good faith that the application of any pact must inspire, as recognized by articles 26 and 31 of the Vienna Convention on the Law of Treaties. If those values did not have a significant purpose of their own, their inclusion in an international standard would be useless.

Some principles of the convention have immediate operative force, according to a number of legal scholars, such as Dr. Agustín Gordillo, who states:

> It is important to emphasize a strong limitation to the administrative discretionality the ICAC incorporates to supranational law, ergo also domestic law: several new current legal principles or concepts, which are mandatory for all national, provin-

cial and municipal public agents, salaried and ad honorem or fee-based. This is particularly true in matters of public contracting, advertising, fairness and efficiency. They are not "words" without legal meaning, they are indisputable legal principles whose breach is a violation of the domestic and supranational legal system.[1]

How Can the Parts of the Convention Be Classified?

As has been seen, from the focus that has been adopted for attacking corruption, the parts of the ICAC may be classified into two major groups: (1) preventive measures and (2) penal measures.

Preventive measures are extremely important. As we have already noted, a suitable system for preventing corruption is worth more than a thousand denunciations. This does not mean playing down penal measures, because the punishment system also acts, in a certain sense, as a preventive measure. All preventive measures are condensed in article III, which in this book has been commented on by their principal drafter in the ICAC, Dr. Richard Werksman.

Penal measures may, in turn, be divided into the obligation to legislate classifications of crimes and the obligation to cooperate internationally.

The obligation to establish classifications of crimes includes those that are absolutely and unconditionally binding on the states, those that are explicitly subordinate to the basic principles of national law, and those that the states have positively valued and are required to legislate in a nonimmediate stage.

Within the obligation to cooperate internationally, we can distinguish assistance and cooperation themselves, and extradition. Assistance and cooperation themselves include information and search for evidence, the seizure of property, the lifting of bank secrecy, etc.

In another type of classification, if the ICAC is focused from the standpoint of binding force, we can distinguish four degrees of obligation: (1) unconditional obligation, which covers the commitment to legislate the acts of article VI (in accordance with article VII), extradition, the exercise of jurisdiction, assistance and cooperation, and all that those imply; (2) the obligation to establish legislation subordinate to basic legal principles, including the commitment to include transnational bribery and illicit enrichment; (3) the obligation to legislate classifications of crimes on which the states have already ruled in favor of their appropriateness and which they will take into consideration depending upon the importance of the occasion; (4) preventive measures, which the states have agreed to consider applying, but which may not cease to be taken into consideration as principles for interpreting existing law.

---

[1] Agustín Gordillo, *Tratado de Derecho Administrativo* [Essay on Administrative Law], vol. 1, 4th ed., c. XVI-12 (Buenos Aires: Fundación de Derecho Administrativo, 1997).

The Convention's Subsequent Operation

The OAS, nongovernmental organizations, academia, and the press have already spread the word throughout the hemisphere about the ICAC and its impact on people's lives. The convention is now fully in force and most countries have ratified it. Many governments have even issued new laws and regulations designed to enforce the agreement, and the OAS has produced model legislation to make that task easier.

The ICAC has set a fine example—one that lent impetus to the OECD's Convention on Combating Bribery of Foreign Public Officials in International Commercial Transactions, signed in December 1997.

For many states, the process of defining new offenses, such as transnational bribery and illegal enrichment, will truly pose a challenge to the ingenuity of their legal minds and the adaptability of their judges.

Preventive measures, such as transparency in government procurement and oversight of the personal wealth of public officials, will always require active participation from business organizations and civil society in general.

Whistleblower protection, so difficult in the countries of Latin America, will require special attention from the Inter-American community through deeper commitments and even mechanisms similar to those provided for in the Pact of San José, Costa Rica, for human rights.

None of these objectives will be met automatically. The operation of the convention in general requires a monitoring mechanism that enables the OAS to evaluate fulfillment of the commitments undertaken.

In May 2001, in Buenos Aires, the signatory countries agreed to such a mechanism, finally approved by the Assembly. The corresponding text appears in appendix C. Presumably, this will not be the convention's only step forward in the coming years.

Meanwhile, under God's watchful eye, the families of the Americas await the benefits—for their children and, perhaps, for the present as well—of a way of freedom that was not designed to deprive them of greater opportunity for health, education, security, and justice.

Chapter Four

The Report of Buenos Aires and the Committee of Experts

Unlike the later OECD Anti-Bribery Convention and Council of Europe Criminal Law Convention, the Inter-American Convention against Corruption does not contain an obligatory mutual evaluation mechanism. The negotiations leading to the adoption of the convention did not include any discussion of such a mechanism. However, the current progress in the implementation of the convention and comparisons between the convention and these other international anticorruption instruments prompted considerable discussion about the need for one.

In June 1999 the United States initially proposed that the OAS General Assembly agree to establish a mechanism for monitoring implementation of the convention. This proposal was greeted with some skepticism, but the General Assembly approved a resolution requesting the Permanent Council's Working Group on Probity and Public Ethics to examine the subject. The Working Group met several times. A number of its members also participated in a nongovernmental international workshop to discuss this issue, organized by Transparency International, the Inter-American Bar Association, and the American University Washington College of Law in Washington, D.C., in November 1999. Subsequently, the Working Group and the Permanent Council proposed, and the OAS General Assembly in June 2000 approved, Resolution AG/RES. 1723, which instructed the Permanent Council:

> To analyze existing regional and international follow-up mechanisms with a view to recommending, by the end of 2000, the most appropriate model that State Parties could use, if they think fit to monitor implementation of the Convention. That recommendation will be transmitted to the State Parties to the Convention for them to choose the course of action they deem most appropriate.

The OAS Committee on Juridical and Political Affairs referred this mandate to the Working Group on Probity and Public Ethics, which convened on September 7, 2000, under the chairmanship of Argentina. The Working Group, open to all OAS members, met on numerous occasions at the OAS Headquarters. The principal contributors to the negotiations were Argentina, Canada, Jamaica, the United States, and Mexico, with additional input from Uruguay, Peru, Brazil, and El Salvador. By late 2000, the Working Group produced a recommendation that called for the creation of a "Committee of Experts" and presented a set of guidelines for an evaluation of the implementation of the convention. The purposes of the mechanism are to promote implementation of the convention, "to facilitate technical cooperation activities, the exchange of information, experience and best practices, and the harmonization of the anticorruption legislation of the States Parties." The Working Group recommended that while the mechanism would be intergovernmental in nature, the Committee of Experts could receive written comments from nongovernmental bodies, "taking into account the Guidelines for the Participation of Civil Society Organizations in OAS activities, as well as the definition of civil society in AG/RES.1661 (XXIX-0/99)." It was agreed that only countries that had ratified the convention would participate in the evaluation process.

On January 18, 2001, the Permanent Council accepted the Working Group's recommendations and transmitted them to the states parties to the convention in Resolution CP/RES.783. The mechanism assigned to the Committee a number of specific duties, including the selection of topics under the convention to be reviewed, countries to be evaluated, and the issuance of a report that will be forwarded first to the states parties and then made public. The Republic of Argentina invited the states parties to meet in Buenos Aires on May 2–4, 2001, for the first informal meeting of the Committee of Experts. The states parties met on March 21–23, 2001, in Washington, D.C., to establish a preliminary framework for the Committee meeting in May. The May meeting produced the Report of Buenos Aires, which was adopted by the foreign ministers of twenty countries in June 2001.

The first formal meeting of the Committee of Experts of the Follow-up Mechanism for the implementation of the convention took place in Washington on January 14–18, 2002. All twenty-two states parties that had by then signed the Report of Buenos Aires sent experts. These states parties representatives reflected a diversity of professional backgrounds, including prosecutors, anticorruption offices, diplomats, and auditors. Several had worked on the Report of Buenos Aires.

To better understand the lessons learned in other evaluation mechanisms, the first day of the meeting opened with briefings by representatives of four other mutual evaluation mechanisms (OECD, Council of Europe, FATF, and the Multilateral Evaluation Mechanism of the Inter-American Drug Abuse Control Commission). The remainder of the week was devoted primarily to Committee deliberations, which produced the "Draft Rules of Procedure and Other Provisions" that were finalized in late February. On the last day, Dr. Carlos Balsa, president of the Anti-Corruption Commission of Uruguay, was selected as the chair for the first year of the mechanism's operation. Consensus was not reached on a vice chair, and it was decided, therefore, to postpone the vice chair selection until the next meeting.

While the Rules track the Report of Buenos Aires quite closely, they do contain key decisions of the Committee in several important areas. First, they limit the term of the chair and vice chair to one-year terms with reelection limited to the next year. The need for flexibility in dealing with the leadership was considered more important than continuity. Second, the Secretariat of the OAS is given major responsibility for initiating documents, including the questionnaire, the methodology, and draft country reports. This reflects confidence in the Secretariat based upon the professional and efficient manner in which the first drafts of the rules of procedure and work plans had been produced by the Secretariat. Third, it was decided that the working languages of the Committee would be the languages of only the participating states parties, which at that time were Spanish and English. It was recognized that when Brazil and Haiti eventually ratify the convention and adopt the mechanism, Portuguese and French will have to be added. Fourth, the Committee recognized the importance of civil societies' involvement. Following the parameters set by the Report of Buenos Aires for Civil Society Organizations' (CSO) participation, "only such entities that have formally registered with the OAS under its procedures for such participation" shall have access to Committee documents and opportunity to comment. In addition, it was the Committee's intent that there be ample dissemination of final Committee documents above and beyond the CSO community. Fifth, site visits were deemed appropriate only when necessary and in the interests of equality. Such visits would occur only if they were going to be made to all state parties in the same round. However, any single state party could still invite a site visit at any time. Sixth, the Committee selected the following as the provisions in the convention that would be the subject of the first-round evaluation: section 1 (Standards of Conduct); section 2 (Mechanisms to Implement the Standards); section 4 (Financial Disclosure Reports); section 9 (Supervisory Anticorruption Offices); and section 11 (Enhancing Civil Society Role in Corruption Prevention) of article III, as well as articles XIV (Assistance and Cooperation) and XVIII (Central Authorities for Assistance and Cooperation). This selection reflected the consensus that the first round should be productive without being overloaded and that cooperation and technical assistance are absolutely essential aspects of the convention.

The topic of financing came up at several times but was purposely omitted from the Rules. It was felt that financing of the Mechanism was a matter for the Conference of the States Parties, and that the chairman and the Secretariat would make the necessary overtures to the Conference. As of the first Committee meeting, only the United States ($50,000), Canada ($50,000), and Mexico ($25,000) had made financial contributions to the Committee's operations. The Secretariat was requested to prepare a budget for the first year of operations of the Committee that would be considered by the states parties.

The second meeting of the Committee took place in Washington, D.C., on May 20–24, 2002. The continuity of participants that was the hope of the first meeting prevailed. All twenty-two states parties sent the same experts who had participated in the first meeting except Bolivia and Nicaragua. The Committee achieved all the goals established for the meeting. First, working on the drafts prepared by the Secretariat, the Committee produced a questionnaire, methodology, and country report outline for the first round. All three of these documents are to be found in the appendixes. While the Committee lauded the Secretariat for preparing a most comprehensive and almost encyclopedic draft questionnaire, the final document approved by the Committee was considerably simpler and shorter.

Second, it selected the order pursuant to which all the states parties would be reviewed in the first round, which according to the work plan also developed would take until the end of calendar 2004, approximately two years from the Committee's first meeting. This order consisted first of the eight countries that volunteered (Argentina, Paraguay, Colombia, Nicaragua, Uruguay, Panama, Ecuador, and Chile) in the order that they volunteered, and then the other fourteen in the order that they ratified the convention. It was decided that the first four volunteer countries would be reviewed in time for the Committee to consider and issue the first country reports at its third meeting, scheduled for January 2003. All states parties would be expected to complete and submit the questionnaires within ninety days, that is, before September 1, 2002. There was no discussion about whether the completed questionnaires would be made public. It was the informal consensus that each state party would have to decide whether to disclose the document.

Third, in accordance with the Rules that had been adopted at the first meeting, the Committee drew lots to determine which two states parties would perform the initial assessment of each states party. The Rules require that at least one assessing state party share the same legal system (code or common law) of the assessed state party.

Fourth, the Committee unanimously elected Jesus Faustino Collado from the Dominican Republic to be the vice chair for the first year of the Committee's activities.

On May 31, the OAS Secretariat placed on the Internet the English and Spanish versions of the three basic documents that had been approved at the second meeting, that is, the questionnaire, the methodology, and the country report outline for the first round. The OAS Secretariat also sent the questionnaire to the states parties with instructions to submit the response by the middle of September. In addition, later in 2002, two more countries, Brazil in July and Belize in August, ratified the convention. Brazil joined four other countries that had already ratified the convention—Granada, Guayana, St. Vincent, and the Grenadines and Suriname—in adopting the Mechanism. This brought the total of Committee members to twenty-seven as of November 2002.

The third meeting of the Committee took place in Washington, D.C., on February 10–14, 2003. The major goal of the meeting was to produce final evaluation reports on the first four countries being assessed. As indicated above, these were Argentina, Colombia, Paraguay, and Nicaragua. This ambitious goal was not met for several reasons. First, after lengthy discussions on the Argentina draft, which was considered first, the Committee decided that the draft reports prepared by the Secretariat, the subgroups, and the assessed states parties were too detailed, were inappropriate in tone, and not user friendly. As a result, a drafting committee was created to rewrite the recommendations section of the Argentina report. Its rewrite was discussed at length in the plenary session and finally accepted on the last day of the meeting. The Secretariat was then instructed to redraft the other three reports to conform in tone and style to the Argentine model which the Committee would then consider at its next meeting. Second, the Committee placed much emphasis on the precedential nature of these first reports and the need to produce the best models possible even if all four reports could not be completed at this meeting. The principle of equity in the Report of Buenos Aires and in the Rules of the Committee would require that all future reports conform to the tone and style of these first products. Third, the Committee spent considerable time dealing with several cross-cutting issues before even reaching the Argentine report. These included the matter of federalism and the reach of the convention below national government levels; how to make recommendations to states parties on particular systems or mechanisms when their only obligation under the convention is "to consider the applicability" of such matters; how to deal with the pervasive shortage of statistics or any means to assess progress in any given area that was revealed in the first four draft reports; the role of civil society in the deliberations of the Committee; and the need for establishing clearer processes for Committee decision making between meetings.

The Committee reelected Carlos Balsa D'Agosto, the lead expert from Uruguay, and Faustino Collado, the lead expert from the Dominican Republic, to their second year in office as chairman and vice-chairman, respectively. The next meeting of the Committee was scheduled for July 14–18, 2003.

On March 5, 2003, the final report for Argentina was posted on the OAS website at www.oas.org/juridico/english/mec_rep_arg.htm.

Challenges to the Committee and the Mechanism Process

The Committee and the Mechanism faced certain challenges as the unprecedented process began to assess progress of the states parties in meeting their obligations under the convention. Undoubtedly others will arise in the course of the process, but a number were obvious from the beginning.

First, the Committee faced the problem arising from different expectations that interested parties had about precisely what the scope and results of the process would be. On the one hand, there were the states parties themselves, particularly the Latin Americans, who saw the process as one aimed primarily at identifying and obtaining the technical assistance and cooperation that they needed to combat corruption in their countries. This focus is reflected in the language of the Mechanism, the Rules, and the priority that was placed upon articles XIV and XVIII of the convention by making theses provisions among the first to be assessed. Their concern that the Mechanism could turn into another certification process or another corruption index is also reflected in the selection of the word "seguimiento" in the title of the Mechanism. It is translated into "follow-up" in English, and the same concern results in the absence of such words as "evaluation," "successful," or "deficient" the basic documents of the Committee.

On the other hand are the public and the civil society organizations and others outside government who view the Mechanism as an evaluation process that will promptly and clearly identify shortcomings in the efforts being taken to implement the convention and bring pressure upon the states parties to make appropriate and timely changes in government practices and procedures. This may also be the impression being conveyed by the press, as reflected in the article that appeared in *The Nation*, in Buenos Aires, on June 5, 2002, which stated, "Corruption in Argentina will be evaluated by experts. . . . In January, in Washington, the results will be announced." (Translated by the authors.) This type of announcement overlooks completely the limited scope of the Committee's efforts and creates the kind of expectations that neither the states parties nor the Committee ever intended.

When one realizes that the first round will deal only with a limited number of the convention's provisions, and will probably take three years to complete, the challenge to the Committee to deal with unreasonable expectations becomes clear. Nevertheless, the Committee had to do the work it had committed itself to do, in a timely and useful manner, to meet the demands it had placed upon itself to assess progress consistent with the Rules and the methodology with an emphasis upon identifying the technical assistance the states parties needed to meet their obligations. Obviously, shortcomings would be identified, but the emphasis was to be upon curing deficiencies and not chastising or castigating.

Another challenge to the Committee has to do with its finances. It must continue to depend upon voluntary contributions from states parties to meet its joint expenses, that is, the costs of its meetings and the costs of the OAS Secretariat in document preparation, translation, and dissemination. The costs of translation were held down in the early stages by limiting the languages to Spanish and English. Since Brazil adopted the Mechanism after the second meeting of the Committee in 2002, it will be necessary to include Portuguese. This will increase Committee operating costs, including the expenses of translation at the Committee meetings and in the processing of Committee documents. If and when Haiti ratifies the convention and joins the Mechanism, it will be necessary to add French and costs will increase again. It was estimated that a four-day conference of the Committee would cost approximately $100,000 just for the direct meeting expenses for translation, materials, and support services. This would not include the costs incurred by the Secretariat in preparing documents and doing the research and analysis required of it by the Committee Rules.

Other challenges, of course, faced the Committee members themselves. These included how effective they would be in getting their governments to respond to the questionnaire in a comprehensive and timely manner; how they would respond to the requests for input from civil society and the nongovernmental organizations in their countries; and how they would influence their governments' decisions on how much information to release from the questionnaire and from the country report, since the Rules are silent on the disclosure of the questionnaire responses and leave it to the discretion of each state party to disclose the country report before the final reports from the entire round are released. As for timely response to the questionnaire, it should be noted that when the OAS sent out a questionnaire in May 2000 to the twenty-two states parties that had ratified the convention at that time, requesting basic information from the states parties related to the convention, only eighteen responded.

In addition, in light of the variety of subject matter being reviewed, even in the first phase of the first round, each Committee member would have to decide when it would be necessary to call upon additional expertise and support from elsewhere in his or her government to do the high-quality review of another states party that was expected. Obviously, not all countries would necessarily have the same depth or variety of expertise, which was one of the problems that the Committee, the OAS, and the states parties would have to work out.

Another test for the Committee and the Mechanism had to be whether the states parties would subscribe to the degree of continuity in Committee membership that would be essential to the success of the process. Since a number of the first Committee lead experts were political appointees, some replacements would be necessary over time. But if there was too much turnover, the momentum and institutional memory necessary for its effectiveness would be lost.

Appendix A

THE INTER-AMERICAN CONVENTION AGAINST CORRUPTION

PREAMBLE

THE MEMBER STATES OF THE ORGANIZATION OF AMERICAN STATES, CONVINCED that corruption undermines the legitimacy of public institutions and strikes at society, moral order and justice, as well as at the comprehensive development of peoples;

CONSIDERING that representative democracy, an essential condition for stability, peace and development of the region, requires, by its nature, the combating of every form of corruption in the performance of public functions, as well as acts of corruption specifically related to such performance;

PERSUADED that fighting corruption strengthens democratic institutions and prevents distortions in the economy, improprieties in government and damage to a society's moral fiber;

RECOGNIZING that corruption is often a tool used by organized crime for the accomplishment of its purposes;

CONVINCED of the importance of making people in the countries of the region aware of this problem and its gravity, and of the need to strengthen participation by civil society in preventing and fighting corruption;

RECOGNIZING that, in some cases, corruption has international dimensions, which requires coordinated action by States to fight it effectively;

CONVINCED of the need for prompt adoption of an international instrument to promote and facilitate international cooperation in fighting corruption and, especially, in taking appropriate action against persons who undertake acts of corruption in the performance of public functions, or acts specifically related to such performance, as well as appropriate measures with respect to the proceeds of such acts;

DEEPLY CONCERNED by the steadily increasing links between corruption and the proceeds generated by illicit narcotics trafficking which undermine and threaten lawful commercial and financial activities, and society, at all levels;

BEARING IN MIND the responsibility of States to hold corrupt persons accountable in order to combat corruption and to cooperate with one another for their efforts in this area to be effective; and

DETERMINED to make every effort to prevent, detect, punish and eradicate corruption in the performance of public functions and acts of corruption specifically related to such performance,

HAVE AGREED to adopt the following
Inter-American Convention against Corruption

ARTICLE I

DEFINITIONS

For the purposes of this Convention:

"Public function" means any temporary or permanent, paid or honorary activity, performed by a natural person in the name of the State or in the service of the State or its institutions, at any level of its hierarchy.

"Public official", "government official", or "public servant" means any official or employee of the State or its agencies, including those who have been selected, appointed, or elected to perform activities or functions in the name of the State or in the service of the State, at any level of its hierarchy.

"Property" means assets of any kind, whether movable or immovable, tangible or intangible, and any document or legal instrument demonstrating, purporting to demonstrate, or relating to ownership or other rights pertaining to such assets.

ARTICLE II

PURPOSES

The purposes of this Convention are:

1. To promote and strengthen the development by each of the States Parties of the mechanisms needed to prevent, detect, punish and eradicate corruption; and

2. To promote, facilitate and regulate cooperation among the States Parties to ensure the effectiveness of measures and actions to prevent, detect, punish and eradicate corruption in the performance of public functions and acts of corruption specifically related to such performance.

ARTICLE III

PREVENTIVE MEASURES

For the purposes set forth in Article II of this Convention, the States Parties agree to consider the applicability of measures within their own institutional systems to create, maintain and strengthen:

1. Standards of conduct for the correct, honorable, and proper fulfillment of public functions. These standards shall be intended to prevent conflicts of interest and mandate the proper conservation and use of resources entrusted to government officials in the performance of their functions.

    These standards shall also establish measures and systems requiring government officials to report to appropriate authorities acts of corruption in the performance of public functions.

    Such measures should help preserve the public's confidence in the integrity of public servants and government processes.
2. Mechanisms to enforce these standards of conduct.
3. Instruction to government personnel to ensure proper understanding of their responsibilities and the ethical standards governing their activities.
4. Systems for registering the earnings, property and liabilities of persons who perform public functions in certain posts as specified by law and, where appropriate, for making such registrations public.
5. Systems of government hiring and procurement of goods and services that assure the openness, equity and efficiency of such systems.
6. Government revenue collection and control systems that deter corruption.
7. Laws that refuse favorable tax treatment for any individual or corporation for expenditures made in violation of the anticorruption laws of the States Parties.
8. Systems for protecting public servants and private citizens who, in good faith, report acts of corruption, including protection of their identities, in accordance with their Constitutions and the basic principles of their domestic legal systems.
9. Oversight bodies with a view to implementing modern mechanisms for preventing, detecting, punishing and eradicating corrupt acts.
10. Deterrents to the bribery of domestic and foreign government officials, such as mechanisms to ensure that publicly held companies and other types of

associations maintain books and records which, in reasonable detail, accurately reflect the acquisition and disposition of property, and have sufficient domestic accounting controls to enable their officers to detect corrupt acts.
11. Mechanisms to encourage participation by civil society and nongovernmental organizations in efforts to prevent corruption.
12. The study of further preventive measures that take into account the relationship between equitable compensation and probity in public service.

ARTICLE IV

SCOPE

This Convention is applicable provided that the alleged act of corruption has been committed or has effects in a State Party.

ARTICLE V

JURISDICTION

1. Each State Party shall adopt such measures as may be necessary to establish its jurisdiction over the offenses it has established in accordance with this Convention when the offense in question is committed in its territory.
2. Each State Party may adopt such measures as may be necessary to establish its jurisdiction over the offenses it has established in accordance with this Convention when the offense is committed by one of its nationals or by a person who habitually resides in its territory.
3. Each State Party shall adopt such measures as may be necessary to establish its jurisdiction over the offenses it has established in accordance with this Convention when the alleged criminal is present in its territory and it does not extradite such person to another country on the ground of the nationality of the alleged criminal.
4. This Convention does not preclude the application of any other rule of criminal jurisdiction established by a State Party under its domestic law.

ARTICLE VI

ACTS OF CORRUPTION

1. This Convention is applicable to the following acts of corruption:

a. The solicitation or acceptance, directly or indirectly, by a government official or a person who performs public functions, of any article of monetary value, or other benefit, such as a gift, favor, promise or advantage for himself or for another person or entity, in exchange for any act or omission in the performance of his public functions;

b. The offering or granting, directly or indirectly, to a government official or a person who performs public functions, of any article of monetary value, or other benefit, such as a gift, favor, promise or advantage for himself or for another person or entity, in exchange for any act or omission in the performance of his public functions;

c. Any act or omission in the discharge of his duties by a government official or a person who performs public functions for the purpose of illicitly obtaining benefits for himself or for a third party;

d. The fraudulent use or concealment of property derived from any of the acts referred to in this article;

e. Participation as a principal, coprincipal, instigator, accomplice or accessory after the fact, or in any other manner, in the commission or attempted commission of, or in any collaboration or conspiracy to commit, any of the acts referred to in this article.

2. This Convention shall also be applicable by mutual agreement between or among two or more States Parties with respect to any other act of corruption not described herein.

ARTICLE VII

DOMESTIC LAW

The States Parties that have not yet done so shall adopt the necessary legislative or other measures to establish as criminal offenses under their domestic law the acts of corruption described in Article VI (1) and to facilitate cooperation among themselves pursuant to this Convention.

ARTICLE VIII

TRANSNATIONAL BRIBERY

Subject to its Constitution and the fundamental principles of its legal system, each State Party shall prohibit and punish the offering or granting, directly or indirectly, by its nationals, persons having their habitual residence in its territory, and businesses domiciled there, to a government official of another State, of any article of monetary value, or other benefit, such as a gift, favor, promise or advantage, in connection with any economic or commercial transaction in exchange for any act or omission in the performance of that official's public functions.

Among those States Parties that have established transnational bribery as an offense, such offense shall be considered an act of corruption for the purposes of this Convention.

Any State Party that has not established transnational bribery as an offense shall, insofar as its laws permit, provide assistance and cooperation with respect to this offense as provided in this Convention.

ARTICLE IX
ILLICIT ENRICHMENT

Subject to its Constitution and the fundamental principles of its legal system, each State Party that has not yet done so shall take the necessary measures to establish under its laws as an offense a significant increase in the property of a government official that he cannot reasonably explain in relation to his lawful earnings during the performance of his functions.

Among those States Parties that have established illicit enrichment as an offense, such offense shall be considered an act of corruption for the purposes of this Convention.

Any State Party that has not established illicit enrichment as an offense shall, insofar as its laws permit, provide assistance and cooperation with respect to this offense as provided in this Convention.

ARTICLE X
NOTIFICATION

When a State Party adopts the legislation referred to in paragraph 1 of articles VIII and IX, it shall notify the Secretary General of the Organization of American States, who shall in turn notify the other States Parties. For the purposes of this Convention, the offenses of transnational bribery and illicit enrichment shall be considered acts of corruption for that State Party thirty days following the date of such notification.

ARTICLE XI
PROGRESSIVE DEVELOPMENT

1. In order to foster the development and harmonization of their domestic legislation and the attainment of the purposes of this Convention, the

States Parties view as desirable, and undertake to consider, establishing as offenses under their laws the following acts:

a) The improper use by a government official or a person who performs public functions, for his own benefit or that of a third party, of any kind of classified or confidential information which that official or person who performs public functions has obtained because of, or in the performance of, his functions.

b) The improper use by a government official or a person who performs public functions, for his own benefit or that of a third party, of any kind of property belonging to the State or to any firm or institution in which the State has a proprietary interest, to which that official or person who performs public functions has access because of, or in the performance of, his functions.

c) Any act or omission by any person who, personally or through a third party, or acting as an intermediary, seeks to obtain a decision from a public authority whereby he illicitly obtains for himself or for another person any benefit or gain, whether or not such act or omission harms State property.

d) The diversion by a government official, for purposes unrelated to those for which they were intended, for his own benefit or that of a third party, of any movable or immovable property, monies or securities belonging to the State, to an independent agency, or to an individual, that such official has received by virtue of his position for purposes of administration, custody or for other reasons.

2. Among those States Parties that have established these offenses, such offenses shall be considered acts of corruption for the purposes of this Convention.

3. Any State Party that has not established these offenses shall, insofar as its laws permit, provide assistance and cooperation with respect to these offenses as provided in this Convention.

ARTICLE XII
EFFECT ON STATE PROPERTY

For application of this Convention, it shall not be necessary that acts of corruption harm State property.

ARTICLE XIII
EXTRADITION

1. This article shall apply to the offenses established by the States Parties in accordance with this Convention.

2. Each of the offenses to which this article applies shall be deemed to be included as an extraditable offense in any extradition treaty existing between or among the States Parties. The States Parties undertake to include such offenses as extraditable offenses in every extradition treaty to be concluded between or among them.
3. If a State Party that makes extradition conditional on the existence of a treaty receives a request for extradition from another State Party with which it does not have an extradition treaty, it may consider this Convention as the legal basis for extradition with respect to any offense to which this article applies.
4. States Parties that do not make extradition conditional on the existence of a treaty shall recognize offenses to which this article applies as extraditable offenses between themselves.
5. Extradition shall be subject to the conditions provided for by the law of the Requested State or by applicable extradition treaties, including the grounds on which the Requested State may refuse extradition.
6. If extradition for an offense to which this article applies is refused solely on the basis of the nationality of the person sought, or because the Requested State deems that it has jurisdiction over the offense, the Requested State shall submit the case to its competent authorities for the purpose of prosecution unless otherwise agreed with the Requesting State, and shall report the final outcome to the Requesting State in due course.
7. Subject to the provisions of its domestic law and its extradition treaties, the Requested State may, upon being satisfied that the circumstances so warrant and are urgent, and at the request of the Requesting State, take into custody a person whose extradition is sought and who is present in its territory, or take other appropriate measures to ensure his presence at extradition proceedings.

ARTICLE XIV

ASSISTANCE AND COOPERATION

In accordance with their domestic laws and applicable treaties, the States Parties shall afford one another the widest measure of mutual assistance by processing requests from authorities that, in conformity with their domestic laws, have the power to investigate or prosecute the acts of corruption described in this Convention, to obtain evidence and take other necessary action to facilitate legal proceedings and measures regarding the investigation or prosecution of acts of corruption.

The States Parties shall also provide each other with the widest measure of mutual technical cooperation on the most effective ways and means of preventing, detecting, investigating and punishing acts of corruption. To that end, they shall foster exchanges of experiences by way of agreements and meetings between competent bodies and institutions, and shall pay special attention to methods and procedures of citizen participation in the fight against corruption.

ARTICLE XV
MEASURES REGARDING PROPERTIES

In accordance with their applicable domestic laws and relevant treaties or other agreements that may be in force between or among them, the States Parties shall provide each other the widest possible measure of assistance in the identification, tracing, freezing, seizure and forfeiture of property or proceeds obtained, derived from or used in the commission of offenses established in accordance with this Convention.

A State Party that enforces its own or another State Party's forfeiture judgment against property or proceeds described in paragraph 1 of this article shall dispose of the property or proceeds in accordance with its laws. To the extent permitted by a State Party's laws and upon such terms as it deems appropriate, it may transfer all or part of such property or proceeds to another State Party that assisted in the underlying investigation or proceedings.

ARTICLE XVI
BANK SECRECY

The Requested State shall not invoke bank secrecy as a basis for refusal to provide the assistance sought by the Requesting State. The Requested State shall apply this article in accordance with its domestic law, its procedural provisions, or bilateral or multilateral agreements with the Requesting State.

The Requesting State shall be obligated not to use any information received that is protected by bank secrecy for any purpose other than the proceeding for which that information was requested, unless authorized by the Requested State.

ARTICLE XVII
NATURE OF ACT

For the purposes of articles XIII, XIV, XV and XVI of this Convention, the fact that the property obtained or derived from an act of corruption was intended for political purposes, or that it is alleged that an act of corruption was committed for political motives or purposes, shall not suffice in and of itself to qualify the act as a political offense or as a common offense related to a political offense.

ARTICLE XVIII
CENTRAL AUTHORITIES

For the purposes of international assistance and cooperation provided under this Convention, each State Party may designate a central authority or may rely upon such central authorities as are provided for in any relevant treaties or other agreements.

The central authorities shall be responsible for making and receiving the requests for assistance and cooperation referred to in this Convention.

The central authorities shall communicate with each other directly for the purposes of this Convention.

ARTICLE XIX
TEMPORAL APPLICATION

Subject to the constitutional principles and the domestic laws of each State and existing treaties between the States Parties, the fact that the alleged act of corruption was committed before this Convention entered into force shall not preclude procedural cooperation in criminal matters between the States Parties. This provision shall in no case affect the principle of non-retroactivity in criminal law, nor shall application of this provision interrupt existing statutes of limitations relating to crimes committed prior to the date of the entry into force of this Convention.

ARTICLE XX
OTHER AGREEMENTS OR PRACTICES

No provision of this Convention shall be construed as preventing the States Parties from engaging in mutual cooperation within the framework of other international agreements, bilateral or multilateral, currently in force or concluded in the future, or pursuant to any other applicable arrangement or practice.

ARTICLE XXI

SIGNATURE

This Convention is open for signature by the Member States of the Organization of American States.

ARTICLE XXII

RATIFICATION

This Convention is subject to ratification. The instruments of ratification shall be deposited with the General Secretariat of the Organization of American States.

ARTICLE XXIII

ACCESSION

This Convention shall remain open for accession by any other State. The instruments of accession shall be deposited with the General Secretariat of the Organization of American States.

ARTICLE XXIV

RESERVATION

The States Parties may, at the time of adoption, signature, ratification, or accession, make reservations to this Convention, provided that each reservation concerns one or more specific provisions and is not incompatible with the object and purpose of the Convention.

ARTICLE XXV

ENTRY INTO FORCE

This Convention shall enter into force on the thirtieth day following the date of deposit of the second instrument of ratification. For each State ratifying or acceding to the Convention after the deposit of the second instrument of ratification, the Convention shall enter into force on the thirtieth day after deposit by such State of its instrument of ratification or accession.

ARTICLE XXVI

DENUNCIATION

This Convention shall remain in force indefinitely, but any of the States Parties may denounce it. The instrument of denunciation shall be deposited with the General Secretariat of the Organization of American States. One year from the date of deposit of the instrument of denunciation, the Convention shall cease to be in force for the denouncing State, but shall remain in force for the other States Parties.

ARTICLE XXVII

ADDITIONAL PROTOCOLS

Any State Party may submit for the consideration of other States Parties meeting at a General Assembly of the Organization of American States draft additional protocols to this Convention to contribute to the attainment of the purposes set forth in Article II thereof. Each additional protocol shall establish the terms for its entry into force and shall apply only to those States that become Parties to it.

ARTICLE XXVIII

DEPOSIT OF ORIGINAL INSTRUMENT

The original instrument of this Convention, the English, French, Portuguese, and Spanish texts of which are equally authentic, shall be deposited with the General Secretariat of the Organization of American States, which shall forward an authenticated copy of its text to the Secretariat of the United Nations for registration and publication in accordance with Article 102 of the United Nations Charter. The General Secretariat of the Organization of American States shall notify its Member States and the States that have acceded to the Convention of signatures, of the deposit of instruments of ratification, accession, or denunciation, and of reservations, if any.

Appendix B

INTER-AMERICAN PROGRAM FOR COOPERATION IN THE FIGHT AGAINST CORRUPTION: RESOLUTION ADOPTED AT THE SEVENTH PLENARY SESSION, HELD ON JUNE 5, 1997

THE GENERAL ASSEMBLY,

HAVING SEEN:

Resolution AG/RES. 1397 (XXVI-O/96), in which the General Assembly decided "to instruct the Permanent Council, through the Working Group on Probity and Public Ethics and taking into consideration the pertinent provisions of the Inter-American Convention against Corruption, the respective national legal systems, the documents presented by the Chair of the Working Group and by the Secretary General, and any other contributions it deems relevant, to draw up a draft program for cooperation in the fight against corruption and submit it to the General Assembly at its next regular session"; and

The report of the Permanent Council on the draft resolution entitled "Inter-American Program for Cooperation in the Fight against Corruption" (AG/doc. 3476/97);

CONSIDERING:

That the Charter of the Organization states in its preamble that "representative democracy is an indispensable condition for the stability, peace and development of the region" and that "juridical organization is a necessary condition for security and peace founded on moral order and on justice";

That the member states, in signing the Inter-American Convention against Corruption, stated, in the preamble, that they were "convinced that corruption undermines the legitimacy of public institutions and strikes at society, moral order and justice, as well as at the comprehensive development of peoples";

That the heads of state and government, meeting at the Summit of the Americas held in December 1994, stated that "the problem of corruption is now an issue of serious interest not only in this Hemisphere, but in all regions of the world" and added that "corruption in both the public and private sectors weakens democracy and undermines the legitimacy of governments and institutions. The modernization of the state, including deregulation, privatization and the simplification of government procedures, reduces the opportunities for corruption. All aspects of government in a democracy must be transparent and open to public scrutiny";

That on March 29, 1996, the Specialized Conference on the Draft Inter-American Convention against Corruption adopted the Inter-American Convention against Corruption, a unique international legal instrument that represents an important step forward in action taken within the purview of the Organization of American States;

That the purposes of the Inter-American Convention against Corruption are to promote and strengthen the development by each of the states parties of the mechanisms needed to prevent, detect, punish, and eradicate corruption, and to promote, facilitate, and regulate cooperation among the states parties to ensure the effectiveness of measures and actions to prevent, detect, punish, and eradicate corruption in the performance of public functions and acts of corruption specifically related to such performance;

That the Organization of American States has also been carrying out other activities to help fight the scourge of corruption, in areas such as the drafting of model laws on illicit enrichment and transnational bribery and the compilation of laws of the member states;

That, in response to the mandate issued by the General Assembly, the Working Group on Probity and Public Ethics has been considering the measures which should be adopted by the Organization of American States to achieve more effective international cooperation in fighting corruption;

That the priority interest shown by member states in pursuing the purposes set forth in the Convention, the activities under way in other international organizations, and the efforts of institutions representing civil society have given impetus to anticorruption requirements and opportunities to which the Organization should respond in an appropriate and timely manner; and

That the Organization of American States is an appropriate forum for exchanging information on the challenges faced by the countries of the region as they fight corruption and for implementing such cooperation mechanisms as the member states consider necessary in this important area,

RESOLVES:

1. To adopt—on the basis of the report of the Permanent Council on the Inter-American Program for Cooperation in the Fight against Corruption (CP/doc.2897/97 corr. 1), which contains the report of the Working Group on Probity and Public Ethics that is attached as an integral part of this resolution—the following:

INTER-AMERICAN PROGRAM FOR COOPERATION IN THE FIGHT AGAINST CORRUPTION

The member states of the Organization of American States (OAS), within the framework of the purposes and principles set forth in the Charter of the Organization, bearing in mind the commitment made by the heads of state and government at the Summit of the Americas in 1994 to fight the scourge of corruption, and on the basis of the provisions of the Inter-American Convention against Corruption, the international legal instrument that serves as the general framework for the commitments assumed by member states, have decided to adopt the following Inter-American Program for Cooperation in the Fight against Corruption, the implementation of which will call for the following measures:

I. In the Legal Area

1. Adopt a strategy, through the Permanent Council and its Working Group on Probity and Public Ethics, to secure prompt ratification of the Inter-American Convention against Corruption.
2. Continue to compile national laws on matters related to fighting corruption and identifying corrupt acts.
3. Conduct comparative studies of legal provisions in the member states, identifying similarities, differences, and any loopholes.
4. Examine the legal definitions of illicit enrichment and transnational bribery on the basis of the work of the Inter-American Juridical Committee, including its proposals on model laws in this area.
5. Identify other avenues toward the drafting of model laws that include the most advanced anticorruption approaches. Such model laws could cover both general and specific aspects of this activity.
6. Begin to draft codes of conduct for public officials, as provided in Article III.1 of the Inter-American Convention against Corruption, as member states so request. Account should be taken here of recent work at the United Nations.

7. Consider the problem of the laundering of property or proceeds derived from corruption, providing for activities allowing the states to criminalize the laundering of property derived from corruption, if they have not already done so, in fulfillment of the commitment assumed under Article VI.1.d of the Inter-American Convention against Corruption.
8. Organize the information produced by these activities, promoting the use of electronic media, so as to make the Organization a source of legal information and, in general, a publicity and training tool for anticorruption efforts.

II. In the Institutional Area

1. Identify public institutions in each member state that are engaged in anticorruption efforts, with special attention to the constitutional structure that sustains and organizes the group of institutions in each case, and the role of each, including the Judiciary, parliaments, comptroller's offices, public prosecutor's offices, institutions of the executive branch, police forces, and any specialized anticorruption bodies in those countries that have established them.
2. Promote the sharing of experience with a view to providing services for improving existing anticorruption institutions and systems.
3. Establish, if possible and advisable, a support system for government institutions charged with fighting corruption, with the participation of the Organization of American States.
4. Determine what the public institutions charged with fighting corruption need in order to carry out their functions more effectively; and provide, at the request of the member states, advisory services relating to existing experience at the institutional level, as well as assistance in training staff at those institutions.
5. Provide advisory services to help member states develop educational programs in the area of ethics and other matters related to the conduct of public officials and members of the private sector.
6. Publicize OAS anticorruption activities, using electronic and all other available media.

III. In the International Area

Implement, if appropriate, a system of consultations by which to share experience and information with the United Nations, the Council of Europe, the Organization for Economic Cooperation and Development, the World Bank, the International Monetary Fund, and the Inter-American Development Bank, among others, so as to enhance the understanding of each organization as it fights corruption, avoid duplication of efforts, and assess the prospects for joint projects.

IV. In Civil Society

In order to create, maintain, and strengthen mechanisms for enlisting civil society and non-governmental organizations in efforts to prevent corruption, under Article III.11 of the Inter-American Convention against Corruption, the following activities are envisioned:

1. Conduct media publicity campaigns to secure the signature and ratification of, or accession to, as appropriate, the Inter-American Convention against Corruption.
2. Share experience on the role of the press in fighting corruption.
3. Make programs to complement the formal education efforts the states might undertake through the educational system to promote the ethical values that underlie the fight against corruption.
4. Identify professional organizations whose activities could be linked to anticorruption efforts, so as to enlist the support of bar associations and associations of accountants and auditors, among others.
5. Establish means of enlisting, maintaining, and strengthening the participation of civil society and non-governmental organizations in anticorruption efforts.

2. To instruct the Permanent Council to supervise the implementation of this Program.

3. To instruct the General Secretariat to implement the measures provided for in this Program, through the Secretariat for Legal Affairs, within allocated resources approved in the program-budget and other resources, and to report to the General Assembly at its next regular session on the measures taken and progress made.

4. To express its special appreciation to the Chair of the Working Group on Probity and Public Ethics, Ambassador Edmundo Vargas Carreño, Permanent Representative of Chile, for an excellent job in making it possible to adopt the Inter-American Program for Cooperation in the Fight against Corruption.

TENTATIVE PLAN OF ACTIVITIES FOR 1997 AND 1998

I. In the Legal Area

1. Prepare and initiate implementation of a strategy to secure the signature and ratification of the Inter-American Convention against Corruption.

2. Continue the compilation of national laws of the member states.
3. Design an electronic system for recording legal information and other data relating to the Organization's anticorruption activities, and enter the data on the laws compiled.
4. Make an approach to the comparative study of national laws, and initiate such studies.
5. Begin compiling codes of conduct for public officials and initiate a comparative study of those codes.
6. Begin to study the problem of the laundering of property derived from corruption.

II. In the Institutional Area

1. Identify the institutions in each member state whose activities are linked to anticorruption efforts.
2. Hold a meeting of national institutions responsible for fighting corruption, at which they will share experience, plan joint actions as necessary to implement the preventive measures provided for in Article III of the Inter-American Convention against Corruption and in model laws on illicit enrichment and transnational bribery, and assess what they need to facilitate their work.
3. Begin preparation of a draft plan for strengthening institutions responsible for fighting corruption, in consultation with member states and with the participation of the institutions themselves.
4. Set up a support system for institutions responsible for fighting corruption.

III. In the International Area

1. Establish mechanisms for sharing information and experience with international agencies that have been engaged in fighting corruption.
2. Establish the basis for defining means of coordination with these other international agencies.
3. Hold a seminar with international agencies involved in fighting corruption, to pave the way for coordinated efforts.

IV. In Civil Society

1. Establish mechanisms for sharing information and experience with private organizations interested in fighting corruption.
2. Identify professional associations whose activities are related to the fight against corruption.

Appendix C

REPORT OF BUENOS AIRES ON THE MECHANISM FOR FOLLOW-UP ON IMPLEMENTATION OF THE INTER-AMERICAN CONVENTION AGAINST CORRUPTION

PREAMBLE

The purpose of the Inter-American Convention against Corruption is to promote and strengthen cooperation among the States Parties and to develop the mechanisms needed to prevent, detect, punish, and eradicate corruption.

Considerable progress has already been made in implementing the provisions of the Inter-American Convention against Corruption at the national level, and significant developments have also taken place at subregional and international levels, especially through the Inter-American Program for Cooperation in the Fight against Corruption.

A mechanism to follow-up on and review how such developments are being implemented and to facilitate cooperation among States Parties and among all member states of the OAS will assist in attaining the objectives of the Convention. This mechanism must take account of the need for gradual progress in attaining those objectives and must support programs for implementation of the Convention pursued by the States Parties.

This mechanism is established in fulfillment of the Plan of Action signed at the Third Summit of the Americas, in Quebec City, Canada, in whose chapter on corruption the Heads of State and Government undertook to support the establishment, as soon as possible, taking into consideration of the recommendation of the OAS, of a follow-up mechanism for the implementation of the Inter-American Convention against Corruption by the States Parties to this instrument.

1. Purposes

The purposes of the mechanism shall be:

a. To promote the implementation of the Convention and contribute to attaining the purposes set forth in Article II thereof;
b. To follow up on the commitments made by the States Parties to the Convention and to study how they are being implemented; and
c. To facilitate technical cooperation activities; the exchange of information, experience, and best practices; and the harmonization of the legislation of the States Parties.

2. Basic Principles

Development of the mechanism for follow-up of the commitments of the States Parties to the Convention shall be guided by the purposes and principles established in the Charter of the Organization of American States. Therefore, the powers accorded to it and the procedures it follows shall take account of the principles of sovereignty, nonintervention, and the juridical equality of the states, as well as the need to respect the Constitution and the fundamental principles of the legal system of each State Party.

3. Characteristics

The mechanism for follow-up of implementation of the Convention shall be intergovernmental in nature and shall have the following characteristics:

a. It shall be impartial and objective in its operations and in the conclusions it reaches.
b. It shall ensure equitable application and equal treatment among States Parties.
c. It shall not entail the adoption of sanctions.
d. It shall establish an appropriate balance between the confidentiality and the transparency of its activities.
e. It shall be conducted on the basis of consensus and cooperation among States Parties.

4. Members of the Follow-up Mechanism

Only States Parties to the Convention shall participate in the follow-up mechanism.

5. Structure and Responsibilities

The follow-up mechanism shall be comprised of two bodies: the Conference of the States Parties and the committee of experts.

All States Parties shall be represented in the Conference. It shall have general authority to implement and responsibility for implementation of the mechanism and shall meet at least once each year.

The committee shall be comprised of the experts appointed by each of the States Parties. It shall be responsible for technical analysis of the implementation of the Convention by the States Parties, among other tasks related to this main function. The Committee may request assistance and guidance from the Conference, which shall meet to consider such requests.

Secretariat services for the mechanism shall be provided by the General Secretariat of the Organization of American States.

6. Headquarters

The headquarters for the follow-up mechanism shall be at the headquarters of the Organization of American States.

7. Activities

a. The Committee shall adopt and disseminate its rules of procedure and other provisions.
b. Country reports
   i. Selection of provisions and methodology

     The committee of experts shall select, from among the provisions of the Convention, those whose application by the States Parties may be reviewed, seeking to maintain general balance among the various types of provision contained in the Convention, and shall determine the length of time it will devote to this task, which shall be known as a "round." The committee shall devise a method for the review of each provision, designed to ensure that sufficient reliable information will be obtained. The Committee shall publish the information referred to in this paragraph.

     At each round, the Committee shall prepare a questionnaire on the provisions selected, based on OAS document CP/GT/PEC-68/00

rev. 3, "Questionnaire on Ratification and Implementation of the Inter-American Convention against Corruption," and shall forward it
to those States Parties to be reviewed. The States Parties shall undertake to reply to the questionnaire by the deadline established by
the committee. The replies to the questionnaire shall be distributed
to all committee members.

ii. Selection of countries

The Committee shall use an impartial method for setting the dates
for review of the information on each State Party, such as their presentation on a voluntary basis, chronological order of ratification of the
Convention, or lot. The Committee shall give adequate advance notice
of the dates for the review of each State Party during each round.

iii. Review of information and preliminary report

To expedite its work, the committee shall establish a subgroup in each
case, comprised of experts from two States Parties, which shall review,
with support from the Secretariat, the information on each State Party.

On the basis of that review, each subgroup shall prepare, with support from the Secretariat, a confidential preliminary report, which shall
be made available to the State Party concerned for its observations.

Each subgroup shall prepare a revised version of the preliminary report, taking into account the observations presented by the State Party
concerned, and present it to a plenary meeting of the Committee for its
consideration.

The plenary meeting of the Committee shall prepare the conclusions
and, if deemed appropriate, make the recommendations it considers
pertinent.

iv. Final report

After completing, at each round, its review of the reports for all
States Parties, the Committee shall issue a final report for each State
Party, containing the observations of the State Party reviewed, which
shall be forwarded first to the Conference and then published.

c. Cooperation

Mindful of the purposes of the follow-up mechanism and in the framework of the Inter-American Program for Cooperation in the Fight against
Corruption, the Committee shall strive to cooperate with all OAS member
states, taking account of the activities already under way within the Organization, and shall report to the Conference thereon.

The Committee shall undertake systematic consideration of the issues
involved in cooperation and assistance among States Parties in order to
identify the areas where technical cooperation is needed and the most
appropriate methods for collection of useful data to review such cooperation and assistance. This work shall take account of the provisions of
Articles XIII through XVI and Article XVIII of the Convention.

d. Observers

States that are not parties to the Inter-American Convention against Corruption may be invited to observe the plenary meetings of the committee of experts if they so request.

8. Civil Society Participation

In order to obtain better input for its review, the Committee shall include in the provisions governing its operation an appropriate role for civil society organizations, taking into account the "Guidelines for the Participation of Civil Society Organizations in OAS Activities" [CP/RES. 759 (1217/99)] and the definition of civil society contained in AG/RES. 1661 (XXIX-O/99), in keeping with the domestic legislation of the State Party under review. The Committee may request information from civil society organizations, for which purpose it shall develop the method it considers most appropriate.

9. Resources

The activities of the follow-up mechanism shall be funded by contributions from States Parties to the Convention, from states that are not parties to the Convention, and from international financial organizations, and by any other contribution that may be received in accordance with the General Standards to Govern the Operations of the General Secretariat, including a specific fund that may be established. Such contributions may include offers by State Parties to organize and host meetings of the bodies of the mechanism. The Conference of States Parties may establish criteria for determining the amounts of regular contributions.

10. Periodic Review of the Mechanism

The Conference shall periodically review the operation of the mechanism, taking account of observations made by the committee of experts, and may introduce such changes as it deems appropriate.

11. Transitory Provision

To facilitate the work of the first meeting of the committee, the Conference considers that topics that the committee might analyze at its first round are, inter alia:

a. Article III, selecting as many measures as the Committee considers appropriate;
b. Article XIV; and
c. Article XVIII.

In the event that the committee of experts encounters difficulties in conducting a review of all topics indicated, it shall report such difficulties to the Conference so that that body may take such decisions as it deems appropriate at its next Conference.

The Conference also suggests that, during its first year of operation, the committee of experts hold at least two meetings.

CONFERENCE OF THE STATES PARTIES, BUENOS AIRES, ARGENTINA— MAY 2 TO 4, 2001

MINUTES OF THE MEETING

On May 2 to 4, 2001, the States Parties to the Inter-American Convention against Corruption met to establish a mechanism for follow-up on implementation of the Convention.

The meeting was held with the participation of delegations from the following States Parties: Argentina, The Bahamas, Bolivia, Canada, Chile, Costa Rica, Dominican Republic, Ecuador, El Salvador, Mexico, Nicaragua, Panama, Paraguay, Peru, United States, Republic of Uruguay, and Venezuela, and with the participation of representatives from the following states not party to the Convention: Brazil, Guatemala, and Haiti. Representatives of the Inter-American Development Bank and the Organisation for Economic Co-operation and Development also participated.

The General Secretariat of the OAS provided secretariat services for this First Conference.

The First Conference is the result of work carried out in the framework of the OAS Working Group on Probity and Public Ethics pursuant to OAS General Assembly resolution AG/RES. 1723 (XXX-O/00). In addition, the recommendations of the meeting of the Group of Experts held in Washington, D.C., March 21 to 23, 2001, pursuant to OAS Permanent Council resolution CP/RES. 783 (1260/01), were the terms of reference considered at the Conference.

As a result of the discussion that took place in Buenos Aires, the First Conference of States Parties reached consensus, details of which are given in the report attached hereto, the "Report of Buenos Aires on the Mechanism for Follow-up on Implementation of the Inter-American Convention against Corruption," which will be submitted to the Conference of the States Parties to the Inter-American Convention for its consideration and possible adoption at the meeting thereof to be held during the thirty-first regular session of the General Assembly of the OAS, in San José, Costa Rica, from June 3 to 5, 2001.

Done in Buenos Aires, on the fourth day of May, 2001.

Appendix D

COMMITTEE OF EXPERTS OF THE MECHANISM FOR FOLLOW-UP ON THE IMPLEMENTATION OF THE INTER-AMERICAN CONVENTION AGAINST CORRUPTION

RULES OF PROCEDURE AND OTHER PROVISIONS

I. SCOPE OF THE RULES OF PROCEDURE AND OTHER PROVISIONS

Article 1. Scope of the Rules of Procedure and Other Provisions. The Rules of Procedure and Other Provisions (hereafter Rules) shall prescribe the structure and operation of the Committee of Experts (hereafter Committee) of the Mechanism for Follow-up (hereafter Follow-up Mechanism) on the Implementation of the Inter-American Convention against Corruption (hereafter Convention).

The Committee shall have the responsibility of undertaking its activities within the framework of the purposes, basic principles, characteristics and other provisions established in the "Report of Buenos Aires on the Mechanism for Follow-up on the Implementation of the Inter-American Convention against Corruption" (hereafter Report of Buenos Aires), of the decisions that are adopted by the Conference of States Parties and, pertinently, of the Organization of American States (OAS) Charter.

The Committee may resolve those matters not addressed by these Rules, the Report of Buenos Aires or the OAS Charter in accordance with the provisions in article 3 (k) and article 13.

II. STRUCTURE AND RESPONSIBILITIES OF THE COMMITTEE

Article 2. Composition. The Committee shall be comprised of the experts appointed by each of the States Parties that are members of the Follow-up Mechanism (hereafter States Parties).

Each State Party shall notify the Secretariat of the name or names and personal information (address, e-mail address, phone and fax number) of the expert or experts that will represent it in the Committee. When more than one expert is appointed, the State Party shall indicate the name of the expert who shall lead the group. In this case, the lead expert shall be the contact point for the Secretariat in distributing documents and for all communications.

Each State Party shall notify the Secretariat when there is a change in its representation to the Committee.

Article 3. Responsibilities of the Committee. In accordance with the Report of Buenos Aires, the Committee shall be responsible for the technical analysis of the implementation of the Convention by the States Parties. In performing this function, the Committee shall undertake the following:

a. Adopt its annual working plan, for which the Secretariat will develop a draft in conformity with the provisions in article 9 (a) of these Rules.
b. Select, from among the provisions of the Convention, those whose implementation by all of the States Parties shall be reviewed, seeking to include both preventive measures and other provisions contained in the Convention, and determine the length of time it shall devote to this task, which shall be known as a "round".
c. Adopt a methodology for the review of the implementation of the provisions of the Convention selected to be reviewed in each round that is designed to ensure that sufficient reliable information is obtained. The adoption of this methodology shall comply with the procedure described in article 18 of these Rules.
d. Adopt a questionnaire on the provisions selected for review in each round, based on OAS document CP/GT/PEC-68/00 rev. 3 "Questionnaire on Ratification and Implementation of the Inter-American Convention against Corruption" and in accordance with article 18 of these Rules.
e. Select, in each round, an impartial methodology (such as presentation on a voluntary basis, in chronological order of ratification of the Convention or by lot) for setting the dates for review of the information on each State Party.

f. Determine the composition of each subgroup, to be comprised of experts from two States Parties in accordance with article 20 of these Rules, which shall review, with support from the Secretariat, the information on the State Party they have been assigned to review.
g. Adopt the country reports in regard to each of the States Parties and a final report at the end of each round, in accordance with articles 21 to 26 of these Rules.
h. Promote and facilitate co-operation among the States Parties, within the framework of the Convention and in accordance with the Report of Buenos Aires and article 36 of these Rules.
i. Approve a yearly activity report, which shall be forwarded to the Conference of States Parties.
j. Review periodically the operation of the Follow-up Mechanism and propose any recommendations it considers pertinent to the Conference of States Parties regarding the Convention and the Report of Buenos Aires.
k. Request the assistance and guidance from the Conference of States Parties, when it considers it necessary or convenient in fulfilling its responsibilities.

Article 4. Chair and Vice-Chair. The Committee shall have a Chair and a Vice-Chair, who will be elected separately from among its members for a one-year term and may be re-elected for the following year.

If the Chair or Vice-Chair cease to serve as representatives of their respective States, then their term as such would be terminated.

If the Chairman ceases to serve as a representative of a State Party or resigns before the term is concluded, the Vice-Chair shall assume the responsibilities of Chair and the Committee shall elect a new Vice-Chair for the remainder of the term.

If the Vice-Chair were to cease serving as a representative of a State Party or resigns before the term is concluded, the Committee shall elect a new Vice-Chair for the remainder of the term.

In the case of a permanent absence of both the Chair and Vice-Chair, their replacements shall be elected during the following Committee meeting, according to the procedure established by these Rules.

Elections of the Chair and Vice-Chair shall be by consensus. In the case of not reaching consensus on the decision it shall be adopted by one half plus one of the lead experts of the States Parties, through a secret vote.

Article 5. Responsibilities of the Chair. The Chair shall have the following responsibilities:

a. Co-ordinate with the Secretariat the various activities related to the operation of the Committee.

b. Open and adjourn all meetings and direct the discussions.
c. Submit to the Committee for its consideration the topics that are a part of the approved order of business for each meeting.
d. Decide on points of order that may arise during deliberations.
e. Put motions to a vote and announce the results thereof.
f. Represent the Committee before the Conference of States Parties, OAS organs and other institutions.
g. Submit to the Committee for its consideration the proposals on the composition of the preliminary review subgroups, to be comprised of experts from two States Parties, which shall review, with support from the Secretariat, the information received from a reviewed State Party.
h. All other responsibilities conferred by these Rules and the Committee.

Article 6. Temporary leave of Chair. When the Chair or Vice-Chair is presiding the Committee, he or she must be excused temporarily from the Chair duties when review and approval of the country report in regards to the State Party he or she represents takes place.

Article 7. Responsibilities of the Vice-Chair. The Vice-Chair shall assume the duties of the Chair in the temporary or permanent absence of the Chair and shall assist the Chair in the performance of his or her activities.

Article 8. Secretariat. The Secretariat of the Committee shall be undertaken by the OAS General Secretariat.

As a result, matters regarding the Secretariat's technical and administrative personnel, as well as its structure and responsibilities, shall adhere to the provisions in the OAS Charter, the General Standards to Govern the Operations of the General Secretariat of the OAS approved by its General Assembly, and the decisions that the Secretary General may adopt in developing said General Standards.

Article 9. Responsibilities of the Secretariat. The Secretariat shall have the following responsibilities:

a. Prepare an annual draft working plan of the Committee, which shall include the respective proposals in regards to the number of States Parties that will be reviewed in said period, the meetings that will be held for such review and a timetable to complement said activities, and submit it to the Committee for its consideration.
b. Send convocation notices for all Committee meetings.
c. Prepare the draft order of business for each Committee meeting.

d. Prepare the methodology and questionnaire proposals for the review of the provisions of the Convention selected, whose application shall be reviewed in a round, and submit them to the Committee for its consideration and approval, in accordance with article 18 of these Rules.

e. Support the subgroups of experts in the process of reviewing the information received from the States Parties and in preparing and presenting the preliminary reports referred to in provision 7 (b) (iii), of the Report of Buenos Aires.

f. Prepare a draft Final Report at the end of each round, submit it to the Committee for its consideration and, once the Final Report is adopted by the Committee, forward it to the Conference of States Parties.

g. Prepare a draft Committee Annual Report and, once said Report is adopted by the Committee, forward it to the Conference of States Parties.

h. Serve as a custodian for all the documents and files of the Committee.

i. Disseminate, through the Internet and by any other means of communication, information and public documents related to the Follow-up Mechanism, as well as the country and final reports of each round, once they are made public in accordance with these Rules.

j. Serve as the central co-ordinating and contact point for the delivery and exchange of documents and communications between the experts, as individuals or as a Committee, with the Conference of States Parties, OAS organs and other organizations or institutions.

k. Notify the Committee members of communications received or submitted to them for their consideration, unless they are significantly beyond the scope of the responsibilities of the Committee or in the case of Civil Society Organizations that do not comply with the requirements or time periods prescribed in article 33 of these Rules.

l. Prepare the minutes of Committee meetings and maintain its files.

m. Update periodically information on the progress made by each State Party regarding the implementation of the Convention, based on the information submitted by them, directly or within the framework of the Committee meetings in accordance with article 30 of these Rules.

n. Prepare or co-ordinate the preparation of research papers, investigations or studies on topics related to the Committee's responsibilities, which shall be submitted to the Committee for its consideration in conformity with article 36 (b) of these Rules.

o. Advise the Chair, Vice-Chair and the Committee members in undertaking their responsibilities when requested.

p. Promote and organize programs of technical co-operation in conjunction with other international co-operation organizations and agencies to support the States Parties in their efforts to comply with the recommendations that are made by the Committee.

q. All other responsibilities that the Committee may assign to the Secretariat or those which may be necessary for the effective fulfillment of its responsibilities.

Article 10. Means for delivery of communications and distribution of documents. In order to facilitate distribution and minimize costs, the communications between the Secretariat and lead experts (and vice-versa), as well as the documents for consideration by them individually, in subgroups or in plenary Committee meetings, shall be forwarded via electronic mail with a copy to be sent to the Permanent Mission of the respective State Party to the OAS.

The responses to the questionnaires by the States Parties, and whatever other documents they or their lead expert may forward for distribution among the Committee members, shall also be forwarded to the Secretariat in an electronic form.

In extraordinary cases, when no electronic version exists of the documents, they shall be forwarded, preferably, via fax and, as a last alternative, via regular mail.

Article 11. Languages. The working languages of the Committee are the languages of the States Parties which are at the same time the official languages of the OAS.

Article 12. Quorum. Quorum for meeting shall constitute the presence of one-half plus one of the lead experts that represent the States Parties.

Article 13. Decisions. As a general rule, the Committee shall make its decisions by consensus.

In those cases where there is a controversy in regards to a decision, the Chair shall undertake the good offices and all the measures at the Chair's disposal in trying to reach a consensus among the Committee members. Once the Chair considers that this path has been exhausted and that a decision by consensus is not possible, the issue shall be put to a vote. In this event, decisions shall enter into force with a vote of two-thirds of the lead experts present, if the issue is with regard to the adoption of a country or final report or the amendment of these Rules. In all other cases, the decision shall enter into force by a vote of one-half plus one of the lead experts present. In this last case, all votes shall be yes, no or be an abstention.

A lead expert shall abstain from voting when the Committee is considering his or her State Party's draft preliminary report.

Article 14. Consultations by electronic means. In periods between meetings, the Committee may consult through electronic means of communication.

Article 15. Observers. In accordance with provision 7 (d) of the Report of Buenos Aires, States that are not States Parties may be invited to observe the plenary meetings of the Committee if they so request.

Article 16. Headquarters. In accordance with provision 6 of the Report of Buenos Aires, the Committee, as an entity, shall have its headquarters at the OAS.

Article 17. Funding. The Committee's activities will be funded in accordance with provision 9 of the Report of Buenos Aires.

III. REVIEW PROCEDURE

Article 18. Selection of provisions, determination of a round and adoption of methodology and questionnaire. The procedure for the selection of the provisions, the determination of a round and the adoption of a methodology and questionnaire for the review of the implementation by the States Parties of the provisions of the Convention, shall be the following:

a. The Committee shall select the provisions of the Convention whose implementation by the States Parties shall be reviewed, seeking to include both preventive measures and other provisions contained in the Convention. This information shall be made public once the Committee selects the respective provisions.
b. The Secretariat shall prepare the methodology and questionnaire proposals for the review of said provisions and shall forward them to the lead experts of all the States Parties and shall publish them via the Internet and by any other means of communication in accordance with article 33, no later than thirty (30) days before the date of the Committee meeting that will consider said methodology and questionnaire.
c. The Committee in plenary shall adopt the final versions of the methodology and questionnaire, and shall determine the length of time it will devote to the review of the implementation by the States Parties of those provisions selected, which shall be known as a round.
d. The final versions of the methodology and questionnaire shall be disseminated by the Secretariat via the Internet and by any other means of communication.

Article 19. Definition of the review process of the States Parties. At the beginning of every round, the Committee shall:

a. Adopt an impartial methodology (such as presentation on a voluntary basis, chronological order of ratification of the Convention, or lot) for setting the dates for review of the information on each State Party.
b. Determine the number of States Parties whose information shall be the subject of review in each meeting so as to complete the round within the planned time frame.
c. Determine, as a minimum and in accordance with the impartial methodology referred to in paragraph (a) of this article, the States Parties whose information shall be the subject of review for the first meeting within the framework of a round.

In the event that in the beginning of a round only the States Parties whose information shall be the subject of review in the next meeting are selected, then in accordance with the impartial methodology adopted for the entire round, the States Parties whose information shall be the subject of review for the following meeting shall be selected.

The information that is referred to in this article shall be made public once the Committee reaches the decisions herein mentioned.

Article 20. Composition of subgroups for the review of the information and the preliminary report. The Committee, based on the proposal prepared by the Secretariat in co-ordination with the Chair, shall determine the composition of the subgroups with experts (one or more) from two States Parties that, with support from the Secretariat, shall review the information and prepare the preliminary reports on each State Party whose information shall be reviewed in the next meeting by the Committee.

In selecting the members of a subgroup consideration shall be given to the historical legal tradition of the State Party whose information shall be the subject of review.

Consideration will be given to avoid the selection, to a subgroup, of experts from a State Party that has been reviewed by the State Party under review in that round.

Each State Party shall endeavor to be part of a subgroup, on at least two occasions in each round.

Article 21. Questionnaire response. Once the final version of the questionnaire is agreed upon, the Secretariat shall forward it, in electronic format, to the State Party whose information shall be the subject of review, through its

Permanent Mission to the OAS, with a copy to the lead expert on Committee of said State Party.

The State Party shall, through its Permanent Mission to the OAS, forward to the Secretariat the responses to the questionnaire, in electronic format, with all the supporting documents, within the time period that the Committee sets in each round.

The lead experts shall take all the necessary measures in ensuring that their respective States Parties respond to the questionnaire within the time period referred to in the previous paragraph.

Article 22. Co-ordinating governmental unit in regard to the questionnaire. In all matters related to the forwarding and response of the questionnaire, each State Party shall identify the co-ordinating governmental unit and notify the Secretariat. The Secretariat shall then register said unit.

Article 23. Procedure for the review of the information and preparation of the preliminary report. Once the responses to the questionnaire are received, the procedure shall be as follows:

a. The Secretariat shall prepare a draft preliminary report;
b. The Secretariat shall forward the draft preliminary report to the corresponding subgroup for its comments;
c. The subgroup shall forward to the Secretariat any comments they may have in regard to the draft preliminary report;
d. The Secretariat shall forward the draft preliminary report and the comments of the subgroup to the State Party under review for clarification;
e. Upon receipt of its draft preliminary report, the State Party being reviewed shall respond to the comments of the subgroup and the Secretariat;
f. On the basis of the responses of the State Party being reviewed to the comments of the subgroup, the Secretariat shall prepare a revised draft preliminary report, which it shall forward to the Committee at least two weeks before the subsequent Committee meeting for consideration.

Article 24. Preliminary review meeting of the subgroup and the State Party under review. The representatives of each reviewed State Party shall meet with the members of the subgroup in charge of the preliminary review and with the Secretariat the day before the beginning of the Committee meeting in which the said preliminary report shall be considered.

This meeting shall have as its purpose the revision or clarification of those areas of the draft preliminary report where discrepancies in regards to its content or form may still exist and establish a methodology for the presentation of the draft preliminary report in the plenary of the Committee.

Based on the information received from the reviewed State Party, the subgroup may agree to change the text of the draft preliminary report or maintain it as is for its presentation to the Committee. The members of the subgroup shall also agree upon the presentation format of their preliminary report to the plenary of the Committee.

Article 25. Consideration and approval of the country report in the Committee. For the consideration and adoption of the report, the Committee shall proceed as follows:

a. The members of the subgroup in charge of the preliminary review shall briefly present the content and scope of the preliminary report.
b. The reviewed State Party shall make a brief statement in regards to the preliminary report.
c. A discussion, open to the Committee as a whole, shall then begin on the preliminary report.
d. The plenary of the Committee may make any specific changes to the preliminary report it considers necessary, prepare the conclusions and, if deemed appropriate, make any recommendations it considers pertinent.
e. In accordance with the spirit of provision 3 (e) of the Report of Buenos Aires, the Committee shall strive to base its recommendations, if any, on the principles of consensus and cooperation.
f. The Secretariat shall revise the report as agreed by the Committee and shall present the revised report to the Committee for its approval.
g. Once the country report is approved in accordance with the provisions mentioned in the previous paragraphs, the reviewed State Party may authorize the Secretariat to publish it, along with the observations they may have presented, via the Internet or through any other means of communication.

Article 26. Final Report. At the end of a round, the Committee shall adopt a final report which shall include the individual country reports in relation to each one of the States Parties and the observations that each of them had to their reports. Likewise, it shall include an overall review that contemplates, among other things, the conclusions that are arrived at in the country reports and the recommendations of a collective nature in respect to following up on the results of said reports, such as the actions that are recommended in consolidating or strengthening hemispherical cooperation on the issues that are referred to in the provisions under consideration in each round or that are closely related to them.

The final report shall be forwarded to the Conference of States Parties and shall subsequently be made public.

Article 27. Documents. In each round the Secretariat shall recommend the format, characteristics and length of the documents that will circulate within the framework of the Committee's responsibilities, allowing each State Party the possibility of providing additional documents it considers to be necessary.

Article 28. Length and format of the country report. All the country reports shall have the same structure. This structure is to be considered and approved by the Committee in the same manner as foreseen in Article 18 in adopting the methodology and questionnaire.

Article 29. Review of new States Parties. Once a State Party becomes part of the Follow-up Mechanism, it shall:

a. Respond to the previously adopted questionnaires.
b. Be reviewed by the subgroup assigned to follow-up on its compliance with the provisions of the Convention that were considered in previous rounds as well as of those that are being reviewed within the framework of the developing round at the moment the State becomes a State Party.

IV. FOLLOW-UP

Article 30. Reports within the framework of the Committee meetings. At the beginning of each Committee meeting, each one of the States Parties shall report on the measures it has adopted, between the previous meeting and the present one, and on the progress it has made in implementing the Convention. The Secretariat shall always include this issue in the draft order of business for each Committee meeting.

Article 31. Follow-up within the framework of future rounds. At the start of a new round, there shall be included as a section within the questionnaire a chapter with specific questions that will enable the review of the progress made by each State Party in implementing the recommendations included in its individual country report adopted in the previous rounds.

Based on the information received on this point, the individual country report shall review the progress made in the implementation of the recommendations adopted in the previous country reports. In this respect, the report may congratulate a State Party on specific progress made or urge it to comply; in those cases where there has been no progress made in regards to previous country reports.

Article 32. Visits for follow-up. In following up on the provisions reviewed and recommendations made within the framework of a round, as part of the methodology and cooperation efforts in accordance with provisions 3 and 7(b)(i) of the Report of Buenos Aires, the Committee may establish visits by the members of the subgroups to all reviewed States Parties in future rounds.

In addition, visits may be undertaken when the reviewed State Party requests said visit.

V. CIVIL SOCIETY ORGANIZATIONS PARTICIPATION

Article 33. Civil Society Organizations participation. Upon the publication of draft questionnaires, instruments of methodology and any other documents which the Committee deems appropriate, civil society organizations, taking into account the Guidelines for the Participation of Civil Society Organizations in OAS activities CP/RES. 759 (1217/99), and in accordance with the internal legislation of the respective State Party, may:

a. Present, through the Secretariat, specific proposals to be considered in the drafting process referred to in Article 18 of these Rules. These proposals should be presented with a copy in electronic format, within a time frame established by the Secretariat, which time frame will be made public.
b. Present, through the Secretariat, documents with specific and direct information related to the questions that are referred to in the questionnaire with respect to the implementation, by a State Party under review, of the provisions selected for review within the framework of a round. These documents shall be presented, with a copy in an electronic format, within the same time period given to the State Party in responding to the questionnaire.

   The Secretariat shall forward the documents that comply with the aforementioned conditions and terms before mentioned, to the State Party under review as well as to the members of the subgroup in charge of the preliminary review.
c. Present proposal documents related to the collective interest issues that the Committee has included in their annual working plan, in accordance with the provision in article 36 (b) of these Rules. These documents shall be presented, through the Secretariat, with a copy in electronic format, no later than a month before the date of the meeting in which the Committee shall consider these issues.

The Secretariat shall forward a copy of these documents to the lead experts via electronic mail.

Article 34. Distribution of documents from civil society organizations. The documents presented by civil society organizations, in accordance with the provisions in the previous article, shall be distributed in the language in which they were presented. Civil society organizations may, along with the document, annex a translation of it in the official languages of the Follow-up Mechanism, in electronic format, for distribution.

The documents presented by civil society organizations that are not in electronic format shall only be distributed among the Committee members during the meeting when their length is no greater than ten (10) pages. If the length is greater than 10 pages, civil society organizations shall forward enough copies to the Secretariat for distribution.

Article 35. Participation of civil society organizations in Committee meetings. The Committee may invite or accept the request from civil society organizations, within the framework of its meetings, to give a verbal presentation of the documents they presented in accordance with the provision in article 33 (c) of these Rules.

VI. COOPERATION

Article 36. Cooperation. Within the framework if its responsibilities, the Committee shall always take into account that the Convention and the Follow-up Mechanism have as their purposes the need to promote and strengthen cooperation among the States Parties for preventing, detecting, punishing and eradicating corruption.

Taking into account the previous paragraph, the Committee:

a. Mindful of the information that it receives from the States Parties for its review of the implementation of the measures foreseen in the Convention and, in its country and final reports, shall prepare specific recommendations on programs, projects and types of cooperation that will allow States to progress in those specific areas that are referred to in the reports or to search for more effective review measures.

b. In addition to the consideration and adoption of the country and final reports in accordance with the procedures prescribed in these Rules, shall also include the consideration of those collective interest issues related to the Committee's responsibilities in trying to determine specific actions that will allow the strengthening of cooperation among them within the framework of the Convention.

In achieving this purpose, may invite specialists to present the results of their research or investigations in specific areas or recommend the preparation of certain studies, researches or analyses that will allow a greater number of review criteria to be available for the consideration of a specific issue.

c. Based on the information received as a result of the review of the implementation of the provisions of the Convention by the States Parties and the issues that are referred to in the previous paragraph, shall consider and prepare recommendations in regards to the areas in which technical cooperation activities; the exchange of information, experience and best practices; and the harmonization of the legislation of the States Parties should be facilitated to promote the implementation of the Convention and contribute to its purposes established in article II.

d. In accordance with the provision 7(c) of the Report of Buenos Aires, and mindful of the purposes of the Follow-up Mechanism and in the framework of the Inter-American Program for Co-operation in the Fight against Corruption, shall strive to cooperate with all OAS Member States, taking account of the activities already under way within the Organization, and shall report to the Conference of States Parties thereon.

Likewise, it shall undertake a systematic consideration of the issues involved in cooperation and assistance among States Parties in order to identify the areas where technical cooperation is needed and the most appropriate methods for the collection of useful data to review such cooperation and assistance. This work shall take into account of the provisions of Articles XIII through XVI and XVIII of the Convention.

VII. ENTRY INTO FORCE AND AMENDMENT OF THE RULES

Article 37. Entry into force, publicity and amendment of the Rules. These Rules shall enter into force upon their adoption by the Committee and the Committee may amend these Rules through the consensus of the lead experts of the Follow-up Mechanism, or in the event that no consensus is reached, these Rules may be amended through a vote of two-thirds of the said lead experts present in favor of said amendment.

The Secretariat shall communicate these Rules to the Permanent Mission to the OAS of each State Party, and shall publish them via the Internet and by any other means of communication.

Appendix E

QUESTIONNAIRE ON PROVISIONS SELECTED BY THE COMMITTEE OF EXPERTS FOR ANALYSIS WITHIN THE FRAMEWORK OF THE FIRST ROUND,1 MAY 24, 2002

INTRODUCTION

The Report of Buenos Aires and the Rules of Procedure and Other Provisions of the Committee of Experts on the Mechanism for Follow-up on the Implementation of the Inter-American Convention against Corruption (hereinafter, as applicable, Report of Buenos Aires, Rules, Committee, Mechanism, and Convention) provide that the Committee shall adopt a questionnaire on the selected provisions to be reviewed in each round.

At its first meeting, held in Washington D.C. from January 14 to 18, 2002, the Committee decided that during the first round it would review implementation by States Parties of the following provisions of the Convention: Article III, paragraphs 1, 2, 4, 9 and 11; Article XIV; and Article XVIII.

In light of the above, this document contains the questions that comprise the questionnaire adopted by the Committee.

---

[1] This questionnaire was adopted by the Committee of Experts of the Follow-up Mechanism for the Implementation of the Inter-American Convention against Corruption, in its second meeting, held May 20 to 24, 2002, at OAS Headquarters, Washington, D.C.

The responses given to the questionnaire shall be reviewed in accordance with the methodology adopted by the Committee, which shall be annexed to this document, and that can also be consulted on the OAS Internet page at the following address: http://www.oas.org/juridico/english/followup_method.htm

The State Party must also, in complying with a Committee decision, prepare a brief description of its legal-institutional system, consistent with its constitutional framework for the introduction of the country report that is prepared as part of the review process.

In accordance with Article 21 of the Rules, the State Party shall forward the response to the questionnaire through its Permanent Mission to the OAS, in an electronic format, along with the corresponding supporting documents, within the period of time established by the Committee.

To this effect, the OAS General Secretariat's e-mail to which the response to the questionnaire must be sent is the following: jgarciag@oas.org Likewise, this e-mail may be used for consultation purposes.

The response to the questionnaire must be forwarded to the Secretariat *no later than August 31, 2002* and, per the recommendation made by the Committee, *the length of the response should not be greater than 25 pages.*

I. BRIEF DESCRIPTION OF THE LEGAL-INSTITUTIONAL SYSTEM

Please briefly describe the legal-institutional system in your country in accordance with its constitutional framework. (A maximum of 2 pages is suggested)

II. CONTENT OF THE QUESTIONNAIRE

Chapter One

Measures and Mechanisms Regarding Standards of Conduct for the Correct, Honorable, and Proper Fulfillment of Public Functions (Article III, 1 and 2 of the Convention)

1. General standards of conduct and mechanisms

a. Are there standards of conduct in your country for the correct, honorable and adequate fulfillment of public functions? If so, briefly describe them and list and attach a copy of the related provisions and documents.

b. Are there mechanisms to enforce compliance with the above standards of conduct? If so, briefly describe them and list and attach a copy of the related provisions and documents.

c. Briefly state the results that have been obtained in implementing the above standards and mechanisms, attaching the pertinent statistical information, if available.

d. If no such standards and mechanisms exist, briefly indicate how your State has considered the applicability of measures within your own institutional systems to create, maintain and strengthen the standards of conduct for the correct, honorable and proper fulfillment of public functions, and mechanisms to enforce compliance, in accordance with Article III (1) and (2) of the Convention.

2. *Conflicts of interests*

a. Are there standards of conduct in your country regarding the prevention of conflicts of interest in the performance of public functions? If yes, briefly describe them, indicating aspects such as to whom they apply and the concept on which they are based, and list and attach a copy of the related provisions and documents.

b. Are there mechanisms to enforce compliance with the above standards of conduct? If so, briefly describe them and list and attach a copy of the related provisions and documents.

c. Briefly state the results that have been obtained in implementing the above standards and mechanisms, attaching the pertinent statistical information, if available.

d. If no such standards and mechanisms exist, briefly indicate how your State has considered the applicability of measures within your own institutional systems to create, maintain and strengthen the standards of conduct intended to prevent conflicts of interests, and mechanisms to enforce compliance, in accordance with Article III (1) and (2) of the Convention.

3. *Conservation and proper use of resources entrusted to public officials in the performance of their functions*

a. Are there standards of conduct in your country that govern the conservation and proper use of resources entrusted to public officials in the performance of their functions? If yes, briefly describe them, indicating aspects such as to whom they apply and whether there are exceptions, and list and attach a copy of the related provisions and documents.

b. Are there mechanisms to enforce compliance with the above standards of conduct? If so, briefly describe them and list and attach a copy of the related provisions and documents.

c. Briefly state the results that have been obtained in implementing the above standards and mechanisms, attaching the pertinent statistical information, if available.

d. If no such standards and mechanisms exist, briefly indicate how your State has considered the applicability of measures within your own institutional systems to create, maintain and strengthen the standards of conduct intended to ensure the proper conservation and use of resources entrusted to public officials in the performance of their functions, and mechanisms to enforce compliance, in accordance with Article III (1) and (2) of the Convention.

4. Measures and systems requiring public officials to report to appropriate authorities acts of corruption in the performance of public functions of which they are aware

a. Are there standards of conduct in your country that establish measures and systems governing the requirement that public officials report to appropriate authorities acts of corruption in public office of which they are aware? If yes, briefly describe them, indicating aspects such as to whom they apply and if there are any exceptions, and list and attach a copy of the related provisions and documents.

b. Are there mechanisms to enforce compliance with the above standards of conduct? If so, briefly describe them and list and attach a copy of the related provisions and documents.

c. Briefly state the results that have been obtained in implementing the above standards and mechanisms, attaching the pertinent statistical information, if available.

d. If no such standards and mechanisms exist, briefly indicate how your State has considered the applicability of measures within your own institutional systems to create, maintain and strengthen the standards of conduct that establish measures and systems governing the requirement that public officials report to appropriate authorities acts of corruption in public office of which they are aware, and mechanisms to enforce compliance, in accordance with Article III (1) and (2) of the Convention.

Chapter Two

Systems for Registering Income, Assets and Liabilities (Article III, 4)

a. Are there regulations in your country establishing methods for registering the income, assets and liabilities of those who perform public functions in certain posts as specified by law and, where appropriate, for making such disclosures public? If yes, briefly describe them, indicating aspects like to whom they apply and when the declaration must be presented, the content of the declaration, and how the information given is verified, accessed, and used. List and attach a copy of the related provisions and documents.

b. Briefly state the results that have been obtained in implementing the above standards and mechanisms, attaching the pertinent statistical information, if available.

c. If no such regulations exist, briefly indicate how your State has considered the applicability of measures within your own institutional systems to create, maintain and strengthen the regulations that establish methods for registering the income, assets and liabilities of those who perform public functions in certain posts as specified by law and, where appropriate, for making such disclosures public, in accordance with Article III (4) of the Convention.

Chapter Three
Oversight Bodies

a. Are there oversight bodies charged with the responsibility of ensuring compliance with the provisions stated in Article III (1), (2) and (4)? If yes, list and briefly describe their functions and characteristics, and attach a copy of the related provisions and documents.

b. Briefly state the results that said oversight bodies have obtained in complying with the previous functions, attaching the pertinent statistical information, if available.

c. If no such oversight bodies exist, briefly indicate how your State has considered the applicability of Article III (9) of the Convention.

Chapter Four
Participation by Civil Society (Article III, Number 11)

1. General questions on the mechanisms for participation

a. Are there in your country a legal framework and mechanisms to encourage participation by civil society and non-governmental organizations in efforts to prevent corruption? If so, briefly describe them and list and attach a copy of the related provisions and documents.

b. Briefly state the results that have been obtained in implementing the above standards and mechanisms, attaching the pertinent statistical information, if available.

c. If no such mechanisms exist, briefly indicate how your State has considered the applicability of measures within your own institutional systems to create, maintain and strengthen the mechanisms to encourage participation by civil society and non-governmental organizations in efforts to prevent corruption, in accordance with Article III (11) of the Convention.

2. Mechanisms for access to information

a. Are there mechanisms in your country that regulate and facilitate the access of civil society and non-governmental organizations to information under the control of public institutions? Is so, describe them briefly, and indicating, for example, before which entity or agency said mechanisms may be presented and under what criteria the petitions are evaluated. List and attach a copy of the related provisions and documents.

b. Briefly state the results that have been obtained in implementing the above standards and mechanisms, attaching the pertinent statistical information, if available.

3. Mechanisms for consultation

a. Are there mechanisms in your country for those who perform public functions to consult civil society and non-governmental organizations on matters within their sphere of competence, which can be used for the purpose of preventing, detecting, punishing, and eradicating public corruption? If so, briefly describe them and list and attach a copy of the related provisions and documents.

b. Briefly state the results that have been obtained in implementing the above standards and mechanisms, attaching the pertinent statistical information, if available.

4. Mechanisms to encourage active participation in public administration

a. Are there mechanisms in your country to facilitate, promote, and obtain the active participation of civil society and non-governmental organizations in the process of public policy making and decision making, in order to meet the purposes of preventing, detecting, punishing and eradicating acts of public corruption? If so, briefly describe them and list and attach the related provisions and documents.

b. Briefly state the results that have been obtained in implementing the above standards and mechanisms, attaching the pertinent statistical information, if available.

5. Participation mechanisms for the follow-up of public administration

a. Are there mechanisms in your country to facilitate, promote, and obtain the active participation of civil society and non-governmental organizations in the follow-up of public administration, in order to meet the purposes of preventing, detecting, punishing and eradicating acts of public corruption? If so, briefly describe them, and list and attach a copy of the related provisions and documents.

b. Briefly state the results that have been obtained in implementing the above standards and mechanisms, attaching the pertinent statistical information, if available.

Chapter Five
Assistance and Cooperation (Article XIV)

1. Mutual Assistance

a. Briefly describe your country's legal framework, if any, that establishes mechanisms for mutual assistance in processing requests from foreign States that seek assistance in the investigation and prosecution of acts of corruption. Attach a copy of the provisions that contain such mechanisms.
b. Has your government presented or received requests for mutual assistance under the Convention? If so, indicate the number of requests that it has presented, explaining how many of them have not been answered and how many have been denied and for what reason; indicate the number of requests that it has received, explaining how many of them have not been answered and how many have been denied and for what reason; mention the average time it has taken your country to answer said requests and the average time in which other countries have responded, and indicate whether you consider these intervals reasonable.
c. If no such mechanisms exist, briefly indicate how your State has implemented the obligation, in accordance with Article XIV (1) of the Convention.

2. Mutual technical cooperation

a. Does your country have mechanisms to permit the widest measure of mutual technical cooperation with other States Parties regarding the most effective ways and means of preventing, detecting, investigating, and punishing acts of public corruption, including the exchange of experiences by way of agreements and meetings between competent bodies and institutions, and the sharing of knowledge on methods and procedures for citizen participation in the fight against corruption? If so, describe them briefly.
b. Has your government made requests to other States Parties or received requests from them for mutual technical cooperation under the Convention? If so, briefly describe the results.
c. If no such mechanisms exist, briefly indicate how your State has implemented the obligation, in accordance with Article XIV (2) of the Convention.
d. Has your county developed technical cooperation programs or projects on aspects that are referred to in the Convention, in conjunction with international agencies or organizations? If so, briefly describe, including, for example, the subject matter of the program or project and the results obtained.

Chapter Six
Central Authorities (Article XVIII)

1. Designation of Central Authorities

a. Has your country designated a central authority for the purposes of channeling requests for mutual assistance as provided under the Convention?
b. Has your country designated a central authority for the purposes of channeling requests for mutual technical cooperation as provided under the Convention?
c. If your country has designated a central authority or central authorities please provide the necessary contact data, including the name of the agency(ies) and the responsible official(s), the position that he or she occupies, telephone and fax numbers, and e-mail address(es).
d. If no central authority or authorities have been designated, briefly indicate how your State will implement the obligation, in accordance with Article XIV (2) of the Convention.

2. Operation of Central Authorities

a. Does the central authority have the necessary human, financial and technical resources to enable it to properly make and receive requests for assistance and cooperation under the Convention? If yes, please describe them briefly.
b. Has the central authority, since its designation, made or received requests for assistance and cooperation under the Convention? If so, indicate the results obtained, whether there were obstacles or difficulties in handling the requests, and how this problem could be solved.

III. INFORMATION ON THE OFFICIAL RESPONSIBLE FOR COMPLETION OF THIS QUESTIONNAIRE

a. State Party_____
b. The official to be consulted regarding the responses to the questionnaire is:
   ( )Mr. _____
   ( )Ms._____
   Title/position:_____
   Agency/office:_____
   Mailing address:_____
   _____
   _____
   Telephone number:_____
   Fax number:_____
   E-mail address:_____

Appendix F

METHODOLOGY FOR THE REVIEW OF THE IMPLEMENTATION OF THE PROVISIONS OF THE INTER-AMERICAN CONVENTION AGAINST CORRUPTION SELECTED WITHIN THE FRAMEWORK OF THE FIRST ROUND,[1] MAY 24, 2002

The Report of Buenos Aires and the Rules of Procedure and Other Provisions of the Committee of Experts on the Mechanism for Follow-up on the Implementation of the Inter-American Convention against Corruption (hereinafter, as applicable, Report of Buenos Aires, Rules, Committee, Mechanism, and Convention) provide that the Committee shall "devise a methodology for the review of the implementation of the provisions of the Convention selected to be reviewed in each round, designed to ensure that sufficient reliable information is obtained".

At its first meeting, held in Washington D.C. from January 14 to 18, 2002, the Committee decided that during the first round it would review implementation by States Parties of the following provisions of the Convention: Article III, paragraphs 1, 2, 4, 9 and 11; Article XIV; and Article XVIII.

---

[1] This Methodology was adopted by the Committee of Experts of the Follow-up Mechanism for the Implementation of the Inter-American Convention against Corruption, in its second meeting, held May 20 to 24, 2002, at OAS Headquarters, Washington, D.C.

In light of the above, this document contains the proposed methodology for the review of the implementation of these provisions by States Parties. To this end, the document refers to the objective of the review in the first round, to its framework, the general and specific criteria used to guide the review, the possibility of follow-up visits, considerations with respect to the scope of the review of each one of the provisions selected, source of information, the review process, and the recommendations and their follow-up.

I. OBJECTIVE OF THE REVIEW WITHIN THE FRAMEWORK OF THE FIRST ROUND

Within the framework of the purposes of the Convention and the Mechanism, the objective of the review in the first round will be to conduct the follow-up of the implementation in each State Party of the selected provisions, by the review of the existence of a legal framework and of other measures for the implementation of each one of the provisions and, in the case it exists, a review of State Party's results and progress.

II. FRAMEWORK FOR REVIEW

The review of the implementation of the provisions selected in the first round shall be conducted within the framework of the provisions of the Convention as well as of the Report of Buenos Aires and the Rules of the Committee.

III. CRITERIA USED TO GUIDE THE REVIEW

In addition to the principles outlined in the Report of Buenos Aires and the Rules of the Committee, information concerning the implementation of the selected provisions of the Convention by States Parties shall be reviewed based mainly on the general and specific criteria described below.

A. General Criteria

The following three criteria shall guide the general and comprehensive review of the implementation by the States Parties of the selected provisions of the Convention:

1. Equal treatment

In accordance with this criterion, and as concerns the review of information on the implementation of the selected provisions of the Convention, all States

Parties shall enjoy equal and consistent treatment. With a view to ensuring compliance with this criterion, in particular, the following precautionary measures shall be adopted in addition to the principles outlined in the Report of Buenos Aires and the Rules:

a) All States Parties shall be reviewed within the framework of the round and in accordance with the same criteria and procedures;
b) The questionnaire shall be the same for all States Parties; and
c) All country reports shall have the same structure.

2. Functional equivalency

The Committee shall review the measures taken by the State Party to implement specific provisions of the Convention to determine whether those measures seek to achieve the obligations and purposes of the Convention.

In this regard, the Committee shall review the information within the specific legal context and system of each State Party and the issue of whether the measures are uniform among the various States shall not be examined, but the Committee shall appreciate the equivalency of the measures in achieving the expressed purposes.

3. Strengthening of cooperation

In accordance with this criterion, the Committee shall review the information received always taking into account that the purpose of both the Convention and Follow-up Mechanism is to promote, facilitate and strengthen cooperation among States Parties in the prevention, detection, punishment and eradication of corruption.

B. Specific Criteria

The implementation by a State Party of each of the selected provisions shall be reviewed based upon the following specific criteria:

1. Level of progress in the implementation of the Convention

Based on this criterion, the Committee shall review the progress made and shall identify the areas, if any, that require progress in the implementation of the Convention.

2. Existence of a legal framework and/or of other measures

The Committee shall determine, based on this criterion, whether a State Party possesses a legal framework and other measures for the implementation of the respective provision of the Convention.

3. Adequacy of the legal framework and/or other measures

If a State Party possesses a legal framework and other measures for the implementation of the respective provision of the Convention, the Committee shall review whether they are appropriate to promote the purposes of the Convention: to prevent, detect, punish and eradicate corruption.

4. Results of the legal framework and/or of other measures

As concerns this criterion, the preliminary review shall attempt to review to what extent objective results have been generated by the application of the legal framework and of other measures existing in a State Party related to the implementation of a respective provision of the Convention.

IV. POSSIBILITY OF FOLLOW-UP VISITS

Within the framework of the first round, implementation of the selected provisions of the Convention will be reviewed with respect to this methodology.

Upon the conclusion of this round and to follow-up on the reviewed provisions and recommendations, the Committee may undertake on-site visits by the preliminary review subgroup to all the States Parties, in the following rounds, in accordance with the provision in Article 32 of the Rules. In this case, within the methodology that is adopted in the corresponding round, the Committee shall determine the reference terms and conditions in undertaking said on-site follow-up visits.

V. CONSIDERATIONS WITH RESPECT TO THE SCOPE OF THE REVIEW OF THE PROVISIONS SELECTED WITHIN THE FRAMEWORK OF THE FIRST ROUND

For the review of the selected provisions of the Convention to be considered in the first round, the following three thematic areas will be kept in mind, as well as the considerations that are formulated in relation with some of the selected provisions.

A. Standards of Conduct and Mechanisms to Enforce Compliance

The first thematic area is divided into two provisions selected by the Committee for review of implementation by States Parties that establish the following:

Article III—Preventive Measures—For the purposes set forth in Article II of this Convention, the States Parties agree to consider the applicability of measures within their own institutional systems to create, maintain and strengthen:

1. Standards of conduct for the correct, honorable, and proper fulfillment of public functions. These standards shall be intended to prevent conflicts of interest and ensure the proper conservation and use of resources entrusted to government officials in the performance of their functions. These standards shall also establish measures and systems requiring government officials to report to appropriate authorities acts of corruption in the performance of public functions. Such measures should help preserve the public's confidence in the integrity of public servants and government processes.
2. Mechanisms to enforce these standards of conduct.

Given the close relationship between these two measures, they shall be reviewed jointly. In this regard, it should be pointed out that, in accordance with paragraph 1 of the above-mentioned Article III of the Convention, these standards of conduct:

a) "Shall be intended to *prevent conflicts of interest*";
b) As well, shall be intended to "*ensure the proper conservation and use of resources* entrusted to government officials in the performance of their functions"; and,
c) "Shall also establish *measures and systems requiring government officials to report to appropriate authorities* acts of corruption in the performance of public functions."

Similarly, it is important to emphasize that, in accordance with paragraph 2 of the same Article III, the mechanisms shall be designed to "enforce these standards of conduct".

Bearing this in mind, the review of the implementation by States Parties of the measures referred to in paragraphs 1 and 2 of Article III of the Convention shall be divided in accordance with the three topics mentioned above.

For each of these thematic areas, consideration shall be given to both the legal framework (paragraph 1 of Article III of the Convention) and the mechanisms (paragraph 2), and the oversight bodies with respect to the selected provisions.

For the review of the standards of conduct intended to prevent conflicts of interests and of the mechanisms to enforce its compliance of these standards, it shall be taken into account whether these standards refer to the various occasions when such conflicts may arise or be observed, which are, prior to taking up the performance of public functions, during such performance and, subsequently, upon cessation of the performance of such functions.

B. Systems for Registering Income, Assets and Liabilities

The second thematic area shall be concerned with the review of the third provision selected by the Committee, which establishes the following:

> Article III—Preventive Measures—For the purposes set forth in Article II of this Convention, the States Parties agree to consider the applicability of measures within their own institutional systems to create, maintain and strengthen: . . .

> 4. Systems for registering the income, assets and liabilities of persons who perform public functions in certain posts as specified by law and, where appropriate, for making such disclosures public.

For the review of the implementation of this measure, consideration shall be given to the legal framework and, if they exist, the oversight bodies related to that framework.

C. Oversight Bodies

In the third thematic area the review of the implementation of Article III (9) of the Convention shall only address that which has to do with the other provisions of the Convention that were selected within the framework of this first round (Article III (1), (2), (4) and (11)).

D. Civil Society Participation

The fourth thematic area shall refer to the review of the implementation of the fifth provision chosen by the Committee, which establishes the following:

> Article III—Preventive Measures—For the purposes set forth in Article II of this Convention, the States Parties agree to consider the applicability of measures within their own institutional systems to create, maintain and strengthen: . . .

> 11. Mechanisms to encourage participation by civil society and non-governmental organizations in efforts to prevent corruption.

For the purposes of the review of the implementation of this provision, in addition to its consideration in general, the following mechanisms may be taken into account:

a) Mechanisms to ensure access to information. - In this regard, mechanisms that regulate and facilitate the access of civil society and non-governmental organizations to information under the control of public institutions shall be reviewed, taking into account that the possibility of obtaining this information is a prerequisite for these organizations to participate in efforts to prevent corruption.

b) Consultative mechanisms. - In this regard, mechanisms that enable those who perform public functions to request and receive feedback from civil society and non-governmental organizations shall be reviewed, taking into account the valuable contribution made by these consultative mechanisms in efforts to prevent corruption.

c) Mechanisms to encourage active participation in public administration. - In this regard, mechanisms that permit the active participation of civil society and non-governmental organizations in public policy and decision-making processes shall be reviewed, as part of the efforts to prevent corruption.

d) Participation mechanisms in the follow-up of public administration. - In this regard, mechanisms that permit the participation of civil society and non-governmental organizations in the follow-up of public administration shall be reviewed, in order to meet the purposes of preventing, detecting, punishing, and eradicating acts of public corruption.

E. Assistance and Cooperation

The fifth thematic area shall refer to the review of the implementation of Article XIV of the Convention in relation to mutual assistance and technical cooperation.

F. Central Authorities

The sixth thematic area shall refer to the review of the implementation of Article XVIII concerning central authorities and the objectives of international cooperation and assistance provided for in the Convention.

VI. SOURCES OF INFORMATION

The review of the implementation of the selected provisions shall be carried out based on the answers to the questionnaire by the respective State Party, documents presented by civil society organizations in accordance with the Rules of the Committee, and any other pertinent information that the Secretariat and members of the Committee may obtain.

VII. REVIEW PROCESS

As regards the review of the implementation by States Parties of the selected provisions of the Convention, the Committee shall follow the process outlined in its Rules, in development of the Report of Buenos Aires.

VIII. COUNTRY REPORT

Comments made by the Committee in the country report shall:

a) Refer to each of the thematic areas into which the report is divided in accordance with the provisions whose implementation is being reviewed.
b) Identify areas in which the State Party has made progress in its effort to implement the Convention and, if there are any, areas in which additional progress is deemed necessary, and make recommendations to the State Party to take necessary further action.
c) Refer to those areas in that the State Party may request or receive technical cooperation or assistance, as well as to the known resources or programs in this field that can be useful for the State Party.
d) Be sufficiently detailed and specific to enable follow-up of the progress on these recommendations in accordance with the provisions of the Report of Buenos Aires, the Rules of the Committee and this methodology.

IX. DOCUMENTS

The responses of the States Parties to the questionnaire and the draft country reports shall be translated into the languages of the Committee.

In compliance with the provision in Article 27 of the Rules, it is recommended that the responses of the States Parties to the questionnaire not exceed twenty-five (25) pages, allowing each State Party to annex the necessary documents it considers appropriate which shall be distributed in their original language. The State Party may also attach the translations of said annexes into the other languages of the Committee for distribution.

Likewise, it is recommended that the country reports not exceed twenty-five (25) pages.

Appendix G

FORMAT FOR THE COUNTRY REPORTS THAT WILL BE PREPARED IN THE FRAMEWORK OF THE FIRST ROUND,[1] MAY 24, 2002

In accordance with the provision in article 25 and 28 of the Rules of the Committee of Experts of the Follow-up Mechanism to the Implementation of the Convention, the format of the country reports that will be prepared in the first round of review, be the following:

INTRODUCTION

In this section, the report shall identify the reviewed State Party, it shall briefly describe its legal-institutional structure in accordance with the constitutional order and reference will be made, to the date of ratification of the Convention and to the date the State became a party to the Mechanism.

I. SUMMARY OF THE INFORMATION RECEIVED

In this section a summary will be done of the information received for the review of the implementation of the selected provisions of the Convention by the corresponding State Party.

---

[1] This document was adopted by the Committee of Experts of the Follow-up Mechanism for the Implementation of the Inter-American Convention against Corruption, in its second meeting, held May 20 to 24, 2002, at OAS Headquarters, Washington, D.C.

II. REVIEW OF THE IMPLEMENTATION BY THE STATE PARTY OF THE PROVISIONS SELECTED

In this section, in accordance with the methodology adopted by the Committee, the implementation by the State Party of the provisions selected in the framework of the first round will be reviewed.

To this effect, this chapter of the country reports will have the following format:

1. Standards of conduct and mechanisms to enforce them (Article III, paragraph 1 and 2)
2. Systems for registering income, assets and liabilities (Article III, paragraph 4)
3. Oversight Bodies (In relation with the selected provisions)
4. Mechanisms to encourage participation by civil society and non-governmental organizations (Article III, paragraph 11)
5. Assistance and Cooperation (Article XIV)
6. Central Authorities (Article XVIII)

In relation with each one of the selected provisions above, within the first round, the following criteria shall be used in accordance with the methodology.

1. Existence of a legal framework and/or of other measures.
2. Adequacy of the legal framework and/or of other measures.
3. Results of the legal framework and/or of other measures.

III. CONCLUSIONS AND RECOMMENDATIONS

In this last section the levels of progress in the implementation of the Convention will be reviewed and in the preparation of the conclusions and recommendations, subgroups and the plenary Committee shall use the criteria established in items III (a), (b) and VIII of the Methodology.

Appendix H

Countries That Have Ratified the Inter-American Convention against Corruption

Country	Signature	Ratification	Deposit with the OAS
Argentina	Mar. 29, 1996	Aug. 4, 1997	Oct. 9, 1997
Bahamas	Jun. 2, 1998	Mar. 9, 2000	Mar. 14, 2000
Barbados	Apr. 6, 2001		
Belize	Jun. 5, 2001	Aug. 2, 2002	Sep. 6, 2002
Bolivia	Mar. 29, 1996	Jan. 23, 1997	Feb. 4, 1997
Brazil	Mar. 29, 1996	Jul. 10, 2002	Jul. 24, 2002
Canada	Jun. 7, 1999	Jun. 1, 2000	Jun. 6, 2002
Chile	Mar. 29, 1996	Sep. 22, 1998	Oct. 27, 1998
Colombia	Mar. 29, 1996	Nov. 25, 1998	Jan. 1, 1999
Costa Rica	Mar. 29, 1996	May 9, 1997	Jun. 3, 1997
D. Republic	Mar. 29, 1996	Jun. 2, 1999	Jun. 8, 1999
Ecuador	Mar. 29, 1996	May 26, 1997	Jun. 2, 1997
El Salvador	Mar. 29, 1996	Oct. 26, 1998	Mar. 18, 1999
Grenada		Nov. 15, 2001	Jan. 16, 2002
Guatemala	Jun. 4, 1996	Jun. 12, 2001	Jul. 3, 2001
Guyana	Mar. 29, 1996	Dec. 11, 2000	Feb. 15, 2001
Haiti	Mar. 29, 1996		
Honduras	Mar. 29, 1996	May 25, 1998	Jun. 2, 1998
Jamaica	Mar. 29, 1996	Mar. 16, 2001	Mar. 30, 2001
Mexico	Mar. 29, 1996	May 27, 1997	Jun. 2, 1997
Nicaragua	Mar. 29, 1996	Mar. 17, 1999	May 6, 1999
Panama	Mar. 29, 1996	Jul. 20, 1998	Oct. 8, 1998

Continued on the next page

Country	Signature	Ratification	Deposit with the OAS
Paraguay	Mar. 29, 1996	Nov. 29, 1996	Jan. 28, 1997
Peru	Mar. 29, 1996	Apr. 4, 1997	Jun. 4, 1997
Saint Vincent & Grenadines		May 28, 2001	Jun. 5, 2001
Suriname	Mar. 29, 1996	Mar. 27, 2002	Jun. 4, 2002
Trinidad and Tabago	Apr. 15, 1998	Apr. 15, 1998	Apr. 15, 1998
United States	Jun. 2, 1996	Sep. 15, 2000	Sep. 29, 2000
Uruguay	Mar. 29, 1996	Oct. 28, 1998	Dec. 7, 1998
Venezuela	Mar. 29, 1996	May 22, 1997	Jun. 2, 1997

Note: All of the ratifying countries listed above have adopted the document of Buenos Aires except Grenada, Guyana, Haiti, and St. Vincent & Grenadines.

Appendix I

Websites for Current Information about the Inter-American Convention against Corruption and Other Related Sources

1. The Convention:
   www.oas.org/juridico/english/Treaties/b-58.html
2. Status of Signers/Ratifications:
   www.oas.org/juridico/english/sig/b-58.html
3. Report of Buenos Aires:
   www.oas.org/juridico/english/followup_corr.arg.htm
4. Rules of Procedure and Other Provisions:
   www.oas.org/juridico/english_rules.htm
5. Questionnaire:
   www.oas.org/juridico/english/questionnaire.doc
6. Methodology:
   www.oas.org/juridico/english/followup_method.htm
7. Country Report Format:
   www.oas.org./juridico/english/followup_format.htm
8. Replies to the Questionnaire:
   www.oas.org/juridico/english/correspen.htm
9. Respondanet, a project funded by USAID:
   www.respondanet.com

10. Transparency International:
    www.transparency.ord
11. Probidad, a daily summary of newspaper reports on corruption in Latin
    America:
    www.probidad.org.sv

About the Editors

CARLOS A. MANFRONI received his law degree from the College of Law and Social Sciences at the University of Buenos Aires. He is a certified fraud examiner whose certificate has been issued by the Association of Certified Fraud Examiners in Austin, Texas. In Argentina, he chairs the Public Ethics Foundation, a non-governmental organization dedicated to preventing corruption. He was a member of the "Group of Experts" who drafted the Inter-American Convention against Corruption at the OAS. He is the director of the postgraduate course "International Rules Against Corruption" at the school of law and political sciences at Universidad Católica Argentina Santa María de los Buenos Aires. He also directed the "World Policies" website (www.worldpolicies.com), a center for international policy data and documents. For three consecutive years—1998, 1999, and 2000—he has received the "Best Legal Book Award," the highest honor granted by the Inter-American Bar Association for works from the Western Hemisphere, for his books *The Inter-American Convention against Corruption—Annotated with Commentary* (in its first Spanish edition, with a chapter written by Richard S. Werksman); *Transnational Bribery*; and *Political Control in Global Capitalism*, all published by Abeledo-Perrot of Argentina. The author is also a consultant on public policy issues for government and private agencies and has given lectures on the Inter-American Convention against Corruption in most of the countries of the Americas. He was the only person invited from his country to the First International Conference on Ethics in Governments, organized by the United States Office of Government Ethics and the United States Information Agency, in Washington, D.C., in November 1994. In 1998 he was named an honorary member of the Inter-American Academy of International and Comparative Law in the Republic of Peru.

RICHARD S. WERKSMAN has been Senior Anticorruption Programs Adviser at the U.S. Department of State since October 1, 1999, when the U.S. Information Agency (USIA) was merged with the State Department. His responsibilities include serving as lead U.S. representative on the Committee of Experts created in 2001 to monitor implementation of the Inter-American Convention against Corruption. He frequently participates in international seminars and conferences as a speaker on preventive measures in the fight against corruption.

He previously served for twelve years as an Ethics Officer at USIA, where he was responsible for the design and implementation of the ethics program, which combined the training and advising of over eight thousand employees and a wide range of federal laws and regulations governing their conduct. He also contributed actively to the USIA's participation in international efforts to strengthen democratic institutions, particularly in the fight against corruption in Latin America.

He collaborated as a member of the U.S. team in developing and negotiating the Inter-American Convention against Corruption of 1996 and was one of the principal authors of article III, "Preventive Measures."

Before going to USIA in 1987, he was head of ethics programs for the U.S. Department of Education, which resulted from the Ethics in Government Act of 1978. He previously spent four years in Puerto Rico as representative of the U.S. Office of Economic Opportunity administering anti-poverty programs.

He is a graduate of Columbia University Law School and Columbia College in New York, where he majored in Government and Spanish.